MANIPULATION FOR BEGINNERS

How to Persuade and Influence People with Manipulation, Mind Control and Dark Psychology

Marisa Leary

© Copyright 2020 by Marisa Leary . All right reserved.

The work contained herein has been produced with the intent to provide relevant knowledge and information on the topic on the topic described in the title for entertainment purposes only. While the author has gone to every extent to furnish up to date and true information, no claims can be made as to its accuracy or validity as the author has made no claims to be an expert on this topic. Notwithstanding, the reader is asked to do their own research and consult any subject matter experts they deem necessary to ensure the quality and accuracy of the material presented herein.

This statement is legally binding as deemed by the Committee of Publishers Association and the American Bar Association for the territory of the United States. Other jurisdictions may apply their own legal statutes. Any reproduction, transmission, or copying of this material contained in this work without the express written consent of the copyright holder shall be deemed as a copyright violation as per the current legislation in force on the date of publishing and subsequent time thereafter. All additional works derived from this material may be claimed by the holder of this copyright.

The data, depictions, events, descriptions, and all other information forthwith are considered to be true, fair, and accurate unless the work is expressly described as a work of fiction. Regardless of the nature of this work, the Publisher is exempt from any responsibility of actions taken by the reader in conjunction with this work. The Publisher acknowledges that the reader acts of their own accord and releases the author and Publisher of any responsibility for the observance of tips, advice, counsel, strategies and techniques that may be offered in this volume.

TABLE OF CONTENTS

Introduction 1
Chapter 1 *Covering The Basics* 2
Chapter 2 *Persuade Or Manipulate* 15
Chapter 3 *Techniques That Tug The Emotional Heartstrings* 27
Chapter 4 *Make Them Agree If You Want Them To* 40
Chapter 5 *Under Your Spell* 52
Conclusion 64
Description 65

INTRODUCTION

Congratulations on purchasing *Manipulation for Beginners* and thank you for doing so.

Edward Bernays once said: *"We are governed, and our minds are molded. Our tastes are formed, and our ideas suggested. All by men that we have never met."* Bernays was the father of modern marketing, and his words sum up perfectly what manipulation involves. Bernays understood that if you wanted to get people to do what *you wanted* them to do, you had to approach them in a different way. He unstood that you cannot present someone with the facts and hope that they would see things in your favor. No, he understood that you had to use the emotional approach. He saw that if you targeted someone's emotions, the decisions they made were less rational, and thus, you could have more control and influence over the things they did.

Manipulators take advantage of other people's emotions. That is how some of the more skilled manipulators so easily wrap other people around their fingers. The most successful manipulators are always the ones you least suspect. If the manipulator does their job right, most people can go on for a long time without ever suspecting what they are up to. Is being a manipulator a bad thing? That depends. There are certain times when a little bit of manipulation could be a good thing, especially if it is done for the greater good. For example, when a parent tries to get their child to be healthy by using subtle manipulation to get them to eat their vegetables. But manipulation could also take on a darker, more sinister side. It depends entirely on what it is used for and the intention behind the manipulation.

Not all forms of manipulation are bad, and if you want to learn the art of getting people to do what you want in a subtle, non-malicious way, you have come to the right place.

There are plenty of books on this subject on the market, thanks again for choosing this one! Every effort was made to ensure it is full of as much useful information as possible, please enjoy!

CHAPTER 1
Covering The Basics

The people in your life manipulate you. Maybe not all of them, but some of them certainly do. They do it so subtly that you don't even realize it is happening until you reflect on it later and say, *"Hang on, something is not quite right here."* Have you ever felt like you were being "tricked" or "forced" into doing something you didn't want to do? But you did it anyway because you felt like you had "no choice but to say yes?". *That is what mental manipulation looks like.*

It's A Mad, Mad, Manipulative World Out There

Call it manipulation or gaslighting; manipulation is a hot topic of discussion because people are finally starting to realize just how frequently it happens. Manipulation is defined as *"controlling or influencing either a person or a situation in a clever and unscrupulous manner, or to control or play upon by means which are unfair or insidious, especially for their own advantage to serve their own purpose."* What makes manipulation such a dangerous thing is that it happens so subtly, sometimes right under our noses, and we could be completely oblivious to it. Someone else could be doing it to you, or you could be the one doing the manipulating. Either way, manipulation is considered a form of emotional and psychological abuse that can be *very harmful* to a person's wellbeing.

Manipulation. It is either happening or has happened to you. It's happening to almost everyone out there in the world today. Manipulators are people who will stop at nothing, who will do, say, and go to any lengths to get what they want. Even if it is at the expense of others. They don't think about how you feel because they're far too concerned about their own selfish needs. It's all about *"me, myself, and I"* when it comes to them. What other people want and need is irrelevant. Manipulators will keep you around as long as they have a need for you, but as soon as you no longer serve their purpose, they will cut you loose. If you were hanging off the side of a cliff with a rope, they would be the ones who cut that rope as soon as you're no longer of any use to them. Sounds brutal and harsh? That is why they call it a form of mental and emotional abuse.

A partner. A Husband. A Friend. A Wife. A Mother. A Brother. A Sister. A Colleague. A Manager. A Supervisor. It could be anyone. Anyone whom you're spending a lot of time with can manipulate you. The first sign to watch out for if you suspect manipulation is afoot is to think about this: *Do you find that you second-guess yourself quite a bit? Do you feel like you can't trust your perception of past events?* If you don't trust your own memories and question whether what you recall actually happened or not, chances are you've been gaslighted or manipulated. Manipulation is a deceptive art, and those who have mastered this art form are referred to as manipulators. Manipulative individuals exist everywhere. You could be a manipulative person yourself.

Why Do They Call It Gaslighting?

This term is based on the 1944 film *Gaslight*. In this movie, the husband of the film's protagonist was the culprit responsible for manipulating her in such a subtle way that she believed she was losing her mind. The movie's name was based on the parts of the film where the husband was the gas lights in the upstairs floor of the flat to dim his own. When the wife brings this up, he manipulates her by trying to convince her that she is imagining it. His persistent misdirection, denial, and contradiction made the wife feel unsure of her sanity. Hence the term gaslighting, a form of emotional and psychological manipulation that is designed to make you feel unsure of your own sanity. Manipulators gaslight when they completely deny reality.

Manipulators will try to distort your thoughts and your reality. Gaslighting is when they try to gain the upper hand by making you question your reality. Manipulators will resort to this tactic when they either want to avoid responsibility, control you, manipulate you, or do all three. If they have to manipulate you to the point where you might think you're going crazy, they'll have no problems doing it through a series of frequent lies. They play games with the victim's mind by basically implying that they "feel this, think that, and thought you experienced it, but you didn't." They make you second-guess yourself by denying, twisting, and discounting everything that you say to make it seem like the victim imagined the whole thing in their mind. They could tell you you're crazy, oversensitive, forgetful, anything to make you question your sanity and your thoughts. They want you to feel like you can't be trusted to make your own decisions. Maybe you've been a victim of gaslighting quite a few times in your life too if any of these statements are starting to sound familiar.

The Signs You're Being Gaslighted

You better believe that if someone is gaslighting you, they are doing it on purpose. They are using this manipulative tactic for a reason, and that reason is often to try and control you. They want to influence your decisions and your actions so they can try to get you to do what they want. They *always* have a hidden agenda of some sort. The worst part is, it's hard to immediately identify who might be a manipulator. On the surface, they make you believe that they're amazing. They make you yearn to be part of their crowd. They make you believe that they love you. They are charming, persuasive, and they draw you into forging some kind of a relationship with them before eventually revealing their true colors.

But underneath it all lies a sinister, underhanded character who has been toying with your emotions all along. They rely on manipulation because they want you to do what they want without saying it outright to your face. They know that if they demand point-blank that you do what they want, you're going to say no right away. That is why they prefer to choose the sneaky, underhanded approach instead.

The signs you can look out for that indicate a gaslighter might be in your presence include the following:

- You don't feel comfortable around certain people. They make you feel like you always have to have your guard up. When you know you have to be in their company, you start to feel knots in your stomach because of how much you're dreading the encounter. You might not be acutely aware that they are manipulative, but there is just something about them that makes you feel uncomfortable either before or after the encounter. Call it a sixth sense, but if your gut is telling you something is amiss, trust your gut. Even if you can't put your finger on it, if you sense something is off, it probably is.
- You feel like you are the one who has to apologize for everything when you're around them. Even if it is not your fault, they have an uncanny way of making you feel guilty when something doesn't go right. They make you worry about "letting them down" or "disappointing them." They have no qualms about making you feel bad for not helping them out, playing on your guilt, and making themselves seem like the injured party in the scenario. To avoid feeling that way, you find that you go out of your way a lot just to make them happy. Even if it is at the expense of your own happiness. Guilt is one of the manipulator's favorite tactics because it is a form of emotional manipulation. Manipulators are skilled at distorting the truth and making themselves seem like the innocent victim in any scenario.
- You find that you seem to sacrifice your happiness a lot for their sake. You put aside your needs *for their sake*. You go out of your way, above and beyond, *for their sake*. Everything is always about them. It feels like your whole life seems to revolve around them, their opinions, and their needs. They love making other people feel bad about themselves. They play on your feelings of guilt to get what they want, and when it isn't given to them, they revert back to being the victim, hoping that you'll feel guilty enough to take the action they wanted you to all along. You may be a caring, thoughtful, loving, and generous person by nature, and you don't mind doing things for others, but around these gaslighters, it feels like you're doing *too much*, and you're not comfortable with that. When you're trying to make sure everyone else is happy all the time, your own happiness ends up taking a back seat.

- You find that you're cautious about everything you say and do when you're around them. Sometimes you find that you hold back and refrain from sharing your thoughts and opinions because you're worried these might be used against you. That is a *sure sign* you're in the presence of a manipulator. If you wanted a loud and clear sign that you might be a victim of gaslighting, this is it. Your interests and feelings will never be as important as their own, and they will always look out for themselves first before anyone else. Since they usually don't like taking blame or responsibility for anything, they will go to extreme lengths to avoid it, including twisting and turning your words and throwing them back in your face.
- They make you feel guilty for talking about your problems. If they were a true friend or confidant, why would they make you feel guilty about wanting to talk about your problems? That is because they don't *want* you to talk about their problems, and they want your attention to be focused on them. By making you feel guilty, this brings the attention back to them. This puts the spotlight back on them. They love playing the victim card. When you tell them you've had a rough day at work, they'll immediately jump in with how their problem today was so much bigger. They make you pity them and *apologize* for the fact that you had a rough day at work.
- They make you feel like there is something fundamentally wrong with you. You can't quite put your finger on it, but every time you're around someone who is trying to gaslight you, there's a sense of unease. Maybe you felt confident 5-minute ago, but as soon as they came, that confidence seems to have vanished into thin air. They make you feel like you're crazy, weak, sensitive, broken, and flawed. If you feel this way, the chances are that you have been a victim of gaslighting.
- They make you feel like you need to look to them for answers because you can't trust your own judgment. If these manipulators stick around in your life long enough, you reach a point where you feel helpless when it comes to making decisions. You feel like you need to depend on them, in a way, for the answers that you seek because they have somehow convinced you that they know better. Don't be fooled, because this is what they want you to think. To get you to see things their way, manipulators will attempt to poison and distort your perception of a person or situation. Sometimes even before you have had a chance to meet the person for yourself, you find that you're already carrying around a biased opinion about them because of what the manipulator has whispered in your ear.

- They make you feel afraid of everything. Richard Nixon once said that people tend to react to fear and not to love. Manipulators love this because they use fear as one of their most powerful weapons at their disposal. They play on your fears and insecurities to get you to bend to their will by sowing the seed of fear in your mind and watering it with their comments until you go along with what they wanted all along. They love playing on your insecurities, and manipulators have an uncanny ability for sussing out situations where you may feel uncomfortable or insecure about, and they pounce on those moments, hoping to take advantage of them. If being criticized in front of others makes you feel insecure, the manipulator is going to take every opportunity they can to belittle you, undermine you, and make fun of you in the presence of others. If making mistakes makes you feel insecure, they will jump at the chance to turn even the simplest mistake and make it seem more disastrous than it really is. If you've been struggling to pinpoint why a certain someone made you feel afraid and on edge when you were around them, this could be the reason why.
- When you think about who you are now, you suddenly realize that you have become a much weaker version of yourself. Compared to the person you were before these manipulators walked into your life, you seem to have gone downhill. When you think about the person you were, you realize that you were a lot stronger before, and since they came into your life, things haven't been good. When you feel like you've become nothing but a shell of your old self, it is a sure sign that you have been (or you currently are) a victim of gaslighting.
- You realize that you have become afraid of expressing your feelings, needs, and wants when you're around them. When you're around them, you would prefer to stay quiet rather than speak your mind. That's what the gaslighter has done to you. They have manipulated you enough that you start to second-guess yourself, and you believe that your needs are not as important or valuable as the needs of others. To be more specific, they have led you to believe that *their needs* matter more than yours. They have you convinced that bending over backward to do them favors is the right way to go.

To the manipulator, pushovers are their favorite kind of people because they know that pushovers are easy targets. Manipulators will seek to gain control over you through negative reinforcement. For example, when they attempt to remove you from a negative situation and then act like they're doing you a favor. They seek to gain control over you by subtly punishing you emotionally and psychologically. This might include the silent treatment, shouting, screaming, swearing, intimidation, guilt-tripping, crying, temper tantrums, sulking, and emotional blackmail.

They might try to gain control over you through partial reinforcement too. They do this by creating a sense of fear and doubt. When the partial reinforcement is negative, they have an easier time influencing you to take a certain action you might regret later by leading you to believe you might risk losing something bigger. An example of positive partial reinforcement, on the other hand, might be in the form of encouraging the victim to carry on with a bad habit that will result in a negative outcome for the victim. A gambler might be encouraged to keep on gambling if they're a victim of partial positive reinforcement by encouraging them to believe they shouldn't pass up the opportunity to win more money.

The Three Major Manipulative Personality Groups

Have you ever heard of the *Dark Triad Personalities?* Well, this triad is basically made up of three distinct and overlapping personalities: *Narcissism, Psychopathy, and Machiavellians.* The term dark personality is used to refer to those with a tendency for errant, sociopathic behavior that lacks empathy for others. Basically, when it comes to manipulative personality types, these are the worst of the worse. In 2002, the University of British Columbia's Delroy L. Paulhus and Kevin M. Williams conducted a study to find out just how similar these three personalities were by comparing the three dark personalities with three psychological aspects. What they discovered was that the correlation patterns were very different. Thus, what Paulhus and Williams concluded was that the dark triad personalities were distinct. Let's dive a little deeper into the difference between these personality types:

- **The Narcissist** – The Narcissists are in love with themselves. This leads them to believe they are entitled, in a way. That the whole world owes them something because they are special and they deserve special treatment. This grandiose self-image leads them to believe that they are superior to everyone else around them. When a narcissist's rosy view of themselves is challenged, they can become abusive and aggressive. In some cases where you might be romantically involved with a narcissistic manipulator, they could even resort to tactics that include sexual abuse or harassment, domestic violence or abuse, and even verbal and emotional abuse. Anything that the narcissist perceives as a threat must be immediately stomped on, in their opinion. Go against them often enough, anger them enough, and they'll resort to calling you names to demean you and drag you down. They will call you names to insult you, make you feel inferior, and undermine your opinions and credibility. Some narcissists even take pride in their behavior under the misguided notion of feeling "powerful" when they see someone else suffer at their hands. Their exaggerated levels of self-esteem make them believe they are the picture of perfection, and to themselves, they are infallible. Depending on the individual in question, the strength of the narcissistic tendencies would vary in strength, with some people having a stronger disposition towards this personality than others. Narcissism is associated with grandiosity, a distinct lack of empathy, egotism, and pride.

- **The Machiavellians** - These tend to be the more manipulative personality types. They are calculating, duplicitous, amoral, and focused on nothing but their self-interest and personal gain. The term *"Machiavellian"* actually originates from Niccolo Machiavelli, a renowned diplomat, and politician who lived in 16th century Italy. Machiavelli became notorious when his book, *The Prince*, was published in 1513. This publication was interpreted as Machiavelli's endorsement of the deceit and cunning that takes place in diplomacy. *The Prince's* reputation as a manual for tyranny seems to be well-deserved. Throughout his book, Machiavelli appears to be entirely unconcerned about morality except insofar as it is harmful or helpful when it comes to maintaining power. For example, when told to consider all atrocities necessary to seize power and commit them in a single stroke to ensure future stability. Oppressing religious minorities and attacking neighboring territories are mentioned in the book as effective ways of occupying the public. Machiavelli advises keeping up the appearance of virtues like honesty and generosity but to be ready to abandon these values as soon as your interests are threatened. The Machiavellians are perhaps the most dangerous of the lot emotionally. If you ever cross paths with a Machiavellian, you should know that they are as manipulative as they come. They'll cheat you and take great pleasure in purposely hurting you, even when there's no real rhyme or reason for them to do it. While they seldom display psychopathic tendencies, some Machiavellians have been shown to display a tendency for narcissism. Machiavellians tend to be cynical, deceptive, exploitative, and focus on their self-interest before anything else. In his book, Machiavelli famously wrote: Everyone sees what you appear to be, but very few know who you really are. Shakespeare used the word "Machiavel" to denote an amoral opportunist.
- **The Psychopaths** - These are more insensitive to the three personality groups. They lack empathy for anyone else, and they will often act without thinking. In other words, they tend to leap before they look. They are callous and impulsive, and they also happen to be the most physically dangerous personality of the

group, resorting to harmful behaviors towards others if they don't get what they want. They don't place any worth on anyone except themselves. People that have this manipulative trait could potentially be serial killers because they are predisposed to not caring about anyone except themselves. They have little to no ability to control their impulses, and this instability could then lead them to perform acts of manipulation. The brain of a psychopath may show potential damage to the frontal lobe, insula, and cerebral cortex. Since the brain's frontal lobe is the part of the brain which regulates ethics, any damage to the frontal lobe could result in possible psychopathic tendencies. Psychopaths are distinguished through their impulsive nature, selfishness, antisocial behavior, callousness, and complete lack of remorse for their actions.

What all three personalities have in common is their association with varying degrees of self-interest, questionable morals, and deception. They will deceive you more than once to try and get their way, and they're not apologetic about it when you confront them. They'll come out of nowhere and start flattering you, showering you with praise and compliment right before casually slipping in favor that they need you to do. They will display a complete lack of remorse and morals for their actions. They will make remarks against you or others that are both callous, derisive, and thoughtless. If they're narcissistic, they'll boast and brag to no end, wanting everyone around them to know just how wonderful they are. They find it difficult to accept that someone could be better at them. When they perceive such individuals to be in their midst, they will work hard at tearing them down or holding them back, just so they can be the ones ahead of the pack once more. They will belittle the accomplishments of others, and they will have a jaded view or perception of the world.

Psychopathy and narcissism have a closer link to each other than narcissism. Quite possibly because narcissism is the only personality trait out of the three that stems from insecurity, all three personalities, however, tend to be morally disengaged. This allows them to behave unethically and not feel any remorse over their actions. All three members of the dark triad group share similar behavior characteristics when they are in various social settings. For example, at work, you might find one of these dark personalities in the form of an entitled boss or a colleague who is not shy about using underhanded tactics to weasel their way to the top. They might be the ones who can't seem to make any genuine connections with the people around them. They have a tendency towards egoism, where they were preoccupied with their own achievements. If they had to accomplish those achievements at the expense of others, they would. They also happen to be psychologically entitled, believing that they were superior to everyone else and therefore entitled to get anything that they wanted. They are preoccupied with their own self-interest and desire to boost either their financial or social status. If they had narcissistic tendencies, they would brag about their own superiority.

All three of the dark personalities behave impulsively at times because they lack empathy and self-control. Some can be more sadistic than others, deriving pleasure from mentally or physically inflicting harm on another. What makes them unpleasant to be around is their spiteful tendencies, and how they were willing to retaliate or harm others even if they had to hurt themselves in the process. It's not uncommon for these manipulative characters to try and play the "victim" card in nearly every situation to gain sympathy, and will do whatever it takes to make you feel sorry for them. Besides their displays of social entitlement, all three of the dark personalities have several different ways of interacting with the people around them. Psychopaths and Machiavellians, for example, tend to be cynical and morally suspicious of others. Narcissists, on the other hand, have a skewed sense of self. They think of themselves as better leaders and believe that they are more empathetic than they really are.

The narcissists are also prone to something called *The Triangulation Dynamic*. This dynamic is created when the narcissist starts to put two people against each other, causing a rift between them so deep that both sides believe the problem lies with the other instead of the narcissist. A narcissistic parent could pit two children against each other. A narcissistic man would pit two women against each other and vice versa. It is an extremely effective technique, and it works well as a distraction, and the narcissists love it because this is what they wanted from the beginning. It keeps the blame off them, while simultaneously feeding into their ego of being "desired" when there are two people fighting for their affections. They take pleasure in the notion of being "fought over," and they take even more pleasure from knowing that they have that kind of control or influence over others. Narcissists crave attention, thanks to their inflated sense of self. They need it to feed into their egos and belief about their own self-importance.

Sociopaths versus Psychopaths

It's easy to confuse between the two if you're not extensively familiar with what these personality traits entail. Both seem to be almost similar, but why is one listed as a dark personality trait and not the other? Sociopaths and psychopaths are both parts of the antisocial personality disorder group, and both share a lack of empathy and moral judgment. Some experts believe that sociopathy and psychopathy tend to be one and the same and group them together, while others would argue that there are significant differences between the two disorders. The outward behavior displayed by sociopaths and psychopaths can be as different as night and day. But what distinguishes between the two personalities is that psychopaths are pathological liars (hence the manipulation). They don't mind lying through their teeth if it means they are going to get what they want. Do they feel guilty about it? Not even a little bit. They are willing to lie and spin any story they can if it is going to benefit their agenda at the end of the day. Psychopaths also tend to be fearless, and they have become so good at mimicking behaviors you can't tell you're dealing with a psychopath right away.

The first impression you get of a psychopath could be negative right away since they actually want to appear intimidating. Perhaps what makes them extremely dangerous is their uncanny ability to mimic the people around them so well. No story illustrates this better than the story of Gary Ridgeway, a perfect example of a psychopath's immense lying skills and an inability to feel empathy and form emotional attachments. Between 1982 and 2001, Ridgeway murdered at least 49 women in Washington, most of his victims being prostitutes or young women who ran away. After he killed them, he would often return to his dumping ground, where he would then have sex with the corpses. Some of the bodies were dumped in the Green River, which earned Ridgeway the name Green River Killer. While he committed some of these horrible crimes, he was married to this third wife at the time. Although he targeted prostitutes because he hated them, he loved his wife and had a good relationship with her. In an interview with his wife after Ridgeway went to prison, she still had difficulty coming to terms with the fact that her husband was a serial killer, even going so far as to describe their life together as "loving and content."

It can sometimes take a long time before a psychopath's true colors are revealed. A psychopath may sometimes resort to another approach by getting you to feel sorry for them. They shift the focus of your attention towards them, their needs, and their so-called "misfortunes." They'll regale you with tales that make you feel sorry for them and feel bad enough for them to shower all your time, and attention is completely devoted to making them "feel better." They will go to any lengths to get the attention they seek, even if they must make up some stories along the way. As we can see from the Ridgeway story, psychopaths are capable of hurting others without any guilt or remorse. This makes psychopathy one of the most dangerous forms of all antisocial behavior since psychopaths can dissociate emotionally from their actions, even if those actions are horrifically terrible. They might try to compensate for this tendency by being skilled actors, charming and persuasive, capable of faking emotions that
they cannot feel. They can play whatever role is required of them to win the trust and manipulate others. They create a veneer of social respectability to hide their dark side and any sinister behavior resulting from it.

A key trait that distinguishes sociopaths is that they tend to have a conscience, albeit a weak one. But it is there, nonetheless. They can be self-centered, but sociopaths do care for others. Psychopaths don't care who they have to hurt to get their way. Sociopaths are not that great at hiding their behavior, which explains why they're not listed in the dark triad manipulative personality group. Manipulators have to be skilled at hiding their agenda, or everyone is going to know what they are up to and stay away from them.

For a sociopath, their indulgence and lack of empathy are pretty obvious and noticeable for those who pay attention to the body language cues. A sociopath is more impulsive, irresponsible, tend to to "live on the fringes of society" according to psychologist Scott Bonn, and they can't settle in one place or hold a job for long If they can find legitimate work for what they need, they may resort to shady activity such as lying, cheating, and stealing from people along the way. Charles Ponzi is one example of a sociopath. Ponzi famously said he "supposedly" immigrated to American with only $2.50 in his pocket in cash and $1 million in hopes and dreams. After he arrived in Boston, he spent several years working odd jobs and led a life of lies that was focused on tricking people into investing in sham corporations. One example is his International Reply Coupon Scheme. He used money from investors to pay other investors. This became the infamous *The Ponzi Scheme,* and it is still used as an example today of what a sociopath is capable of.

Who Are They?

No one likes being manipulated. But there are some people out there who deserve an award for how good they are at the art of deception. Sometimes, their victims could go for years without ever realizing that they are being manipulated, like the example of Gary Ridgeway. Although skilled at hiding their true colors, if you know what to look out for, you can spot a manipulator before they have time to do too much damage. Here are some signs to watch out for that alert you to their presence:

- **Attention-Seekers** - Demanding constant attention from you is one of the many typical behaviors of a manipulator. They give off the impression that they are weak, "helpless," and always in need of your help. However, this approach puts them in a powerful positive in the lives of whom they have come to depend on. By acting helpless, they stroke the ego of the people that they depend on, which allows the manipulators to gain a sense of control, but they can quickly become nasty if someone were to resist their request for help or a favor. They won't respect your space and will continually demand attention, even when you have made it obvious that their request is going to inconvenience you.

- **Emotional Blackmail** - They have an uncanny ability to make you feel guilty without actually demanding outright that you do what they want. This tactic is known as emotional blackmail. When you're faced with this situation, they put you in a tough spot, and it makes you feel like you're being forced to do things against your will. They bank on the fact that you're going to feel guilty not being a good friend or partner to them, and they use the emotional blackmail approach to fulfill their own agendas.
- **Indirect Communicator** - They're always sneaky, and they will have something up their sleeves all the time. They will rarely tell you what they are thinking because they want to avoid being caught out. It is important that nothing tarnishes their "good person" image, and they would rather talk about you behind your back than to your face.
- **The "Poor Victim"** – This is a classic and favorite manipulative tactic. In almost every situation, these manipulators will always feel sorry for themselves, and they want others to feel sorry for them too. They seek out sympathy, and they don't mind turning people against each other in order to do it. The thing about these manipulators is they will be the ones who start the fight, yet will end up twisting and turning the entire situation around so that they end up the "victim." When it comes to playing the victim, the manipulator is an expert at seeming small and defenseless, even when nothing could be further from the truth. Don't be fooled by their fake innocence.
- **The All or Nothing Ultimatum** - to get you to go along with what they want, they force you into a corner by giving you an ultimatum that often leaves you no choice but to side with them. Someone who genuinely loved you or cared about you would never make you resort to such a thing. They would never put pressure on you to give up something they know that you loved, or that meant a lot to you. If the manipulator in your relationship doesn't like your friends, they could make you choose between being with them or giving up your friendship. They make you feel pressured into choosing them by instilling the fear that you might lose them if you don't. This type of manipulation can even occur in friendships, where your manipulative friend who might be jealous of a new friendship that you formed makes you choose one or the other.
- **Their Problems Matter More** - Your problems will always be trivial compared to theirs. They will always attempt to minimize your problems by comparing it to theirs. Combined with their talent for playing the victim, they can quickly make you feel guilty for bringing up your issues, even when you had a valid reason to do so. They love making other people feel bad about themselves.

They play on your feelings of guilt to get what they want, and when it isn't given to them, they revert back to being the victim hoping that you'll be guilty enough to take the action they wanted you to all along.

CHAPTER 2
Persuade Or Manipulate

In many circumstances, you'll find that persuasion is a handy trick that will prove useful to you. Being a persuasive person is one of the most useful skill sets you can master. You could use it to coax your boss into giving you the raise you know you deserve, persuade a client to seal the deal, persuade a friend to try out that new restaurant you know they will love, getting your partner or friends to see your point of view, there is so much you could accomplish when you learn how to become just a little more persuasive. But hold on, isn't persuasion almost the same thing as manipulation?

Defining and Understanding Persuasion

Before we can understand the differences that separate manipulation from persuasion, we need to understand what persuasion means. We persuade people around us all the time, and we are clearly doing it with our own self-interest in mind. Persuasion, on its own, is not evil. It is simply a means by which we interact with the people around us. You persuade a friend to meet up with you after work for a drink because you need someone to talk to, even when you know that friend may be tired after a long day at the office. You persuade your teammates to with your approach on a project at work because you know your way is the more efficient one.

Every day, we speak. We utter thousands of words, but do we ever give those words much thought? There is a quote that goes: *Handle them carefully, for words are more powerful than atom bombs*. When words are used and spoken in the right way, they can literally get anyone to do anything that you want them to. Words have the power to change the human mind. Words influence the way we think, how we interpret the information that we receive, and words have an impact on the way we formulate and come to a decision. The way that you choose to present information could sometimes be the difference between gaining a new friend and turning them away completely. Two people who could be similar in every way could have very different results when they try to achieve success. The one who achieves success is often the one who knows how to make every word count. The one who happens to be *more persuasive.*

When you speak the right combination of words, it speaks directly to a person's subconscious. When used correctly, this technique can be used to triumph over lies. By nature, human beings are a curious species. We are often in search of answers and truths. We want to know why things work the way they do, and we have always been in search of answers for as long as we can remember. We ask questions, we discuss, we argue, we explore philosophy, science, even art just to get the answers we desire.

When your view conflicts with that of someone else's, we fall into a game of persuasion, bouncing ideas and facts back and forth as each party tries to convince the other that they are right. The subconscious mind is only able to process yes and no answers, and it tends to make decisions quickly using a few key phrases. That is why the right combination of words and speaks in the way the subconscious mind works can make you instantly more influential and persuasive.

Aristotle wrote a book called *Rhetoric*. In his book, he laid out what he believed to be the three foundations for the art of persuasion, and all three of these foundations distinctly show why persuasion is *not the same thing* as manipulation. In the first foundation, Aristotle believed that persuasion had an element of credibility. He believed that we tend to be more easily persuaded if we believe the person to be trustworthy. Aristotle claimed that a trustworthy person should have three qualities about them, and these were good morals, good sense, and goodwill. When we believe that someone has good moral character when we trust that they will do the right thing, we believe that a person has goodwill when we believe that they have no ulterior motive. A person comes across as having good sense when we believe that we can trust their judgment, and believe that they are rational thinkers who are capable of staying calm and collected.

The second foundation was emotion. When making a decision, we would like to think that people, in general, use all the information available to them to make an informed, unbiased decision. The reality, though, is not the case. People are emotional, and they make decisions primarily based on emotions most of the time. Depending on how we feel at the time, we may be more or less inclined to agree with the other party if we're in the right emotional state at the time of discussion. One way to be as persuasive as you can be is by effectively tapping into their emotions. It is often the way that you make someone feel that leaves the strongest impression. They may forget what you've said, but they'll never forget the way you made them feel. The third foundation, according to Aristotle, was logic. People are more easily convinced when the logic is both strong and easy to follow. To be more persuasive, you have to put forth a sound logical argument. A conclusion is made based on the premises of your argument. These are definitely not traits you would find if manipulation was present.

But Is Persuasion *Manipulative?*

Yes, it sure is. But the thing is, *persuasion is okay*. Yes, it is manipulative, but it's not the far end of the manipulation spectrum where it's all bad news. Persuasion is the *good kind* of manipulation. While manipulation is not going to win you any friends, persuasion can. It can turn your prospective customers into long-term clients. It can turn fans into super fans. Persuasion skills that are used for the right reason can bring about a lot of benefits. Unlike manipulation, where the only person getting something out of it is the one who is doing all the manipulating. A master persuader is someone who knows how to turn a "no" into a "yes," and how to do it without having to lie, cheat, or backstab anybody. But persuasion that is overused can quickly spill over into manipulative territory, so we need to be a little careful right there. There's a very fine, sometimes blurry line that separates the two, and it is when we understand the very definition of what these two terms mean can we begin to distinguish when we may be crossing the line from persuasion and manipulation.

Think of manipulation and persuasion as close relatives, if you will. The easiest way to know if you're crossing over into manipulative territory is when you try to get the other person to do something that is of interest *to you*. You don't really care if it is an inconvenience to them or if it's obvious they don't want to do it. All you care about is your own interest, and you want it done no matter who you have to push to do it in the 4th century BC. Aristotle, the father of persuasion, found himself opposing a group of teachers who were referred to as the Sophists. These Sophists were infamous for their rhetorical teachings, and Aristotle found himself butting heads with these groups of individuals over the fact that the Sophists did not seem to care about truth at all, and they were willing to promote just about any idea for a price. Aristotle firmly believed that the Sophists were engaging in manipulative behavior since there was an apparent intention to deceive others. If there is a genuine desire to help another, and that is the only reason why you may be forcing someone to do something they don't want to do, that could be considered an acceptable form of manipulation.

When it's persuasion, it is usually in the interest of both parties. Everyone hopefully gets to benefit from persuasion and not just you alone. Persuasion still gives people the freedom to choose between whether they want to reject or accept the idea which is being presented to them. Yes, you are trying to move them to side with your point of view, but you're not bullying, begging, or pushing them to do it. Persuasion is trying to convince others by carefully framing your arguments, and by presenting supporting evidence while leaving it up to them to make the final decision on where they stand. It is a *mild form* of manipulation if you really need to compare. Another thing about persuasion is that it is *only effective when you take the time to get to know the other person*. What motivates them? What drives them? What pains them? The most effective and persuasive people out there are the ones who know their audience. When they know who their target audience is, they tailor their messages to fit the needs of the audience. They know that if they want to gently sway their audience and convince them to change their minds, they need to speak to their hearts, not their heads.

If you don't know who your audience is, you cannot persuade them. If you don't know who your audience is, *but* you still try to get them to do what you want, you're manipulating. If your intention is not in the best interest of someone else, then what you are doing is being manipulative. This is quite difficult to do since we are naturally programmed to think about ourselves and our needs first before we think about anyone else's needs. Unfortunately, this is something which happens far too often, and if you suspect you could be on the receiving end of this behavior, take a good look at whether the outcome is benefiting you, or just the manipulator alone. Manipulators don't usually have the best intentions because they don't see others as equal to them. The only thing they care about is their agenda, and everything else comes secondary.

People are not resistant to change. We're adaptable as a species. We're not resistant to change, but we do resist *being changed*. We resist when we think we are being forced to go along with someone else's agenda. We resist when we think someone else is trying to control us. Manipulators may be successful at forcing people to get what they want, but it comes at a price. They never build genuine relationships once people realize what they are up to. Nobody likes being told they are wrong. Nobody likes having their beliefs and opinions rebuked, and all its flaws laid out in detail. When someone tries to prove you wrong, most people would become defensive and attempt to walk away, hoping to never see you again. Persuasion is not about winning or proving that you know better. If you take this approach, you're never going to achieve any kind of success, even if you happen to be right.

If you want to become a more persuasive person, you need to focus on using your skills for good. Focus on what you can do to make someone else's life a little bit better or a little bit easier. Think about what you can do for them that might brighten their day. Persuasion could be a good thing because, at its very core, it is the pursuit of the truth. Through the right amount of persuasion, change for the better can take place. A lot of the good work that gets done today would not be possible without persuasion in play. When used in the right way, persuasion will never be as damaging or detrimental as manipulation is. For example, persuasive messages that are delivered in the form of campaigns that encourage us to quit smoking or donate blood to help save lives. The right kind of persuasion can be responsible for uniting nations and forging peace agreements. Charities and fundraising organizations rely on persuasion to help them raise awareness and drive the donations that they need to continue with their charitable work. Parents rely on persuasion to teach their children about safe and stranger danger. If you want to be persuasive, you need to think about what the nature of your intention is. Do you think about the other person and how they could benefit from it too? Or are you only thinking about yourself and nothing else? Whether you're persuading or manipulating, it all boils down to your intention.

Psychology Tricks Commonly Used to Persuade Anyone

When you want to use it, it can come in handy if you know a few psychological tricks that could help you easily persuade others to go along with what you want, especially when you're faced with someone who has strong opinions and can be difficult to convince. Persuasion is like a healthy debate. You're presenting someone with the reasons why they should agree with you and come over to your side. There's no sneakiness and no blatant deception at play. You're simply presenting the facts and justifying them with supporting evidence while leaving the rest up to the listener to draw their own conclusions.

This is why certain psychological tricks work so well in the game of persuasion. You're simply telling them the facts, and then leaving the final decision up to them, hoping that you have convinced them enough to make the right choice at the end of the day. The power of *choice* is the one that makes the biggest difference of all. With persuasion, you're not forcing someone to take action. There's no *"do this or else"* approach that makes them feel like they have no choice but to do what you ask. Persuasion is situational. The techniques that work well in one context might not be as effective in another. To pull it off, you're going to have to rely on a multitude of communication skills. To appear more persuasive and less manipulative, you could employ the following tactics:

- **Explaining Why You're Making the Request** - Although technically we don't owe anyone an explanation for why we want to do something, there are moments when explaining why you're making a request could help your cause. For example, when you're waiting in a long line at the supermarket but you're in a rush because you have another appointment to get to. Explaining your reasons for getting ahead of everyone else in the queue might make them more willing to let you do it if they knew you had a valid reason. When your reason is compelling enough, people are a lot more likely to listen to your point of view. Perhaps even agree with you if they can empathize and put themselves in your shoes. The bigger your request, the more compelling your reason should be.
- **Be Polite** - Politeness is a quality that gets overlooked so many times. When was the last time you thought about the importance of being polite? There are only two words in the English language that can work magic when you're trying to persuade the people around you. Those words are *please* and *thank you*. People are more open to requests than they are to instructions. If you demonstrate politeness with your requests every step of the way, you are 100% more likely to get other people to say yes to you. Nobody likes to feel like they are forced to do something. They

don't like feeling like they had no choice in the matter. A simple please and thank you alongside your requests, combined with a genuine smile, can work wonders.

- **Be Honest When You're Presenting Your Facts** - Since persuasion is not about spinning lies in the hopes of pulling the wool over someone else's eyes, you're going to be focusing on facts when you try to influence others. You need to present *both* sides of the coin, good and bad, happy and sad. This approach works well because it respects the fact that your audience knows there are two sides to every viewpoint. The next time you're listening to a speech by an influential individual, notice how they present an opposing viewpoint or two instead of just sticking solely to why their argument is right. They know audiences are more likely to be persuaded when you address their concerns and provide solutions to ease their worries. What you're presenting may be focusing on the benefits, but at the same time, by presenting both points of view, you're not disregarding the other side of the story, and your audience is going to appreciate this. Persuasive people use this approach all the time, they talk about the benefits of their argument, acknowledge the potential negative outcomes that could come as a result of their approach, and then once more discuss how beneficial their idea can be in mitigating the problems.
- **Listen Actively** - The most effectively persuasive people you will ever meet are the ones who are active listeners. Listening is a very important part of becoming a more persuasive person. You see, when you're trying to persuade someone, you're trying to get them to listen to your ideas or get their consent. To get them to *accept* your requests, however, the ability to listen is going to serve you well. When you listen actively, it helps you understand the person that you are trying to persuade. This is where you find out what worries, reservations, or objections they might have to your request or proposal. When you know what might be holding them back, you can begin working on phrasing or wording your requests in such a way that they become more appealing. In the game of persuasion, listening is going to trump talking every single time.
- **Compliment Them** - When it comes to the art of persuasion, compliments can go a long way toward helping your cause. People love to be complimented, even if they won't admit it out loud to themselves. The minute you offer someone a genuine compliment, they immediately become open and receptive to what you have to say. That is the opening you've been waiting for to slowly wedge your request in the door. A compliment can be extremely effective in changing someone's preconceived notions

about you. But this only works if the compliment is sincere. It's not going to work if they feel like you are trying too hard. For this tactic to work, you need to make sure that your compliments are both subtle and honest at the same time. An insincere compliment can quickly backfire and have the opposite effect of what you hoped it would do.

- **Using Speech That Is Fluid** - When you're trying to persuade, confidence is the key to winning. When your sentences are colored with hesitant words, like *hmm, ummm, like, I mean,* for example, it gives the impression that you're not as confident. It makes the listener feel as though you're not sure what you're talking about. When speech is fluid, it gives the impression of being confident and self-assured. The more confident you appear to be in your speech, the easier it is going to be for you to persuade others.
- **Faster Speech** - Another persuasive trick is to talk at a faster rate when you're trying to convince someone of what you want. When you're speaking quickly, the person that you're speaking too doesn't have enough time to properly process every single piece of information you're giving them. They might not be able to soak in everything that you're saying to them, and this is an opportunity for you to quickly swing things in your favor. When they don't have enough time to process all the information, they don't have enough time to pick apart your points. Persuasive people make it a point to know who their audience is, and if they know they're going to be in the presence of those who are likely to disagree with them, they adjust the rate of their speech and talk faster. They do the opposite when they know the crowd they're addressing is more likely to agree with what they're saying. When you talk faster and fluidly, it gives the appearance of confidence too. People will be more inclined to listen to what you have to say when you give the appearance that you confidently know what you are talking about.
- **Repeat Their Words** - Another psychologically persuasive trick is to repeat the words that the other person is saying to you. Not everything, of course, you don't want to give the impression of being a copycat or a parrot, mimicking everything that they say. The purpose of repeating some of the things they say to you gives them the impression that you're listening. That you are acknowledging that their opinions matter enough for you to take them seriously. This makes them happy, and when they are happy, they're easily persuaded. Making anyone that you're talking to happy by giving the impression you're paying attention to them will help establish a bond between the two of you, even if you have just met. That rapport will open their minds to the

requests or favors you need to ask of them. Psychologists have been known to use this tactic a lot when communicating with their patients to get them to relax. Be careful not to overuse this tactic, though. You don't want to come across as being weird.

- **Nod Along** - Another quick trick to get people to think you're paying attention to them is to nod along when they're talking. The best persuaders know what an effective technique nodding can be. Robert Cialdini, author of *Influence: The Psychology of Persuasion*, says feeling similar to someone is one of the six most powerful factors in the art of persuasion. Sharing something in common or feeling similar puts two people in sync, which then allows for the pacing and leading of conversation. Two people who are in sync often mirror each other, moving in the same way or even thinking the same thoughts sometimes. Nodding occasionally lets them know that you're affirming the things that they say. It makes them feel supported, and without even realizing it, they'll find themselves being open and receptive to what you have to say in return. Reaffirming nods from you make the other person subconsciously more accommodating and agreeable too.
- **Invest in Getting to Know Them** - If you only approach them whenever you need something, eventually, the person is not going to be very receptive to your requests anymore. They'll think that the only time you ever truly make an effort or come and talk to them is when you want something. That is never a good impression. Successful persuasion calls for balance. When you take, you must be willing to give back in return. You need to be willing to invest the time and energy, developing a rapport with them instead of flat out trying to shove your request in their face right away. You need to demonstrate respect for what they say and never belittle them, even if you happen to disagree with their ideas. You need to get them to *trust* you enough to listen to you with an open mind. One of the best techniques to subtly encourage trust is to mirror them. Use the same tone of voice, the same mannerisms, and the same gestures that they use. The mirror technique inspires confidence when you use the same language that they are using. It makes them feel like you really understand them, and they will eventually begin to trust you. Meet them on their level and show that you're willing to listen, not just make demands all the time.
- **Be Humble, Be Kind** - As keen as you may be to persuade someone to go along with what you want, always maintain honesty and never fudge the truth just to get what you want. That's crossing the line to manipulation and deception when you do that. Simple acts of kindness will go a long way, and

they will be remembered when the time comes, and you happen to need to persuade someone to help you out. It also goes a long way towards building trust by showing that you genuinely care about the way that they feel and that you want them to be happy with the agreed-upon outcome. Always be honest and transparent in your attempts to persuade others. Once they find out that they can't trust you, or that you have misled them in any way, you'll find it hard to convince anyone ever again when the bond of trust has been broken. Each time you show gratitude towards others, express your thanks, treat them with respect, and do favors or lend a helping hand to those who happen to need it most, you win their trust.

- **Do Them A Favor** - When you do someone a favor, most of the time, they will feel obligated to return the favor. Unless they happen to be manipulators who only care about themselves. The best kind of favors are the unexpected ones, and if you do something genuinely nice for someone else, they'll return the favor when the time comes. That time is when you need to persuade them to do something for you. The give and take dynamic is one of the most powerful persuasive techniques. Sometimes you don't even have to say a lot. All you have to do is be nice and promote a relationship based on give and take. When you are nice to others, they'll do the same for you. That way, you're less likely to be rejected when it is time to put forth your requests.
- **Offer A Beverage** - If you're trying to persuade someone over coffee, lunch, dinner, breakfast, or any occasion where food and drink might be present, a subtle persuasive technique you could use is to offer that person a drink. Even better if it is a warm drink like coffee or tea. Offering someone a warm drink psychologically projects feelings of warmth toward you, the person who offered them the beverage. This makes them feel like you are someone who is likable and welcoming.
- **Employ the Contracts Technique** - A method that is used in bargaining, the contrast technique is when you make a demand that is higher than what you actually want. Gradually, you "bargain down" to what you wanted, and it tricks the other person into thinking they're getting a better deal. The huge contrast between the first demand and the last demand is the winning formula. In their minds, the lower offer is a lot more ideal and doable than the first one, which means they will be more inclined to say yes to you.
- **Let Them Think You Can Walk A Mile in Their Shoes** - The secret to successful persuasion is by focusing on how or what you can do to be helpful to other people. Your ability to step into

their world, think what they think, feel what they feel, and be empathetic, that's going to be the key to transforming the relationships that you start to form with them. Most people tend to focus on how they persuade someone else enough to get them to do what they want, when instead what they should be focusing on is how they can be helpful. See the situation from their point of view. If the roles were reversed, what would you need to hear from them in order to convince you? When you try to convince them from an angle that highlights how beneficial it is going to be in resolving a problem or issue that they may be having, or even if it addresses a certain need that they want, it becomes much easier to get them to go along with your agenda. People want to see what's in it for them, and when you can show them the ways they will benefit from your approach, they'll be more than happy to hop over to your side without question.

- **Timing Is Everything** - If you play your cards right and time it well, you can work the situation in your favor. A little interesting fact about people is that they tend to be a lot more agreeable when they are mentally tired. If you know your request might not be well received right away, a little trick you could use is to try and persuade them after they have done something that demanded a lot of mental energy. Even if you can't get them to respond right away, they will at least be willing to listen to your demands. This technique will depend heavily on the person in question, and it's not always going to work. But it is something to keep in mind in your endeavor to be more persuasive. It never hurts to try.

Key Phrases to Winning Them Over

With a few key phrases, you can quickly become a more persuasive person *without* the need to be overly manipulative. You will find it a lot easier to get people to agree with you or go along with what you want in general. Words can be a powerful force of good when used for the right reasons, but on the other end of the spectrum, it can be used not only to control another but to inflict great harm and pain. The phrase the pen is mightier than the sword stems from the very real fact that words can cause a great deal of pain and leave scars so deep they might never fully recover. But if you used your words wisely, you could become an immensely powerful, influential person without having to force anyone to do your bidding.

What are these power phrases? These are by far the best that you can start with:

- **I'm Not Sure If It's for You** - Add the word "but" at the end of that sentence, and it will allow you to introduce an idea easily and in a clever, unsuspecting manner. The other person is not going to realize what you're doing at all because they will be too preoccupied, thinking about what you just said. When you say something like, *"I'm not sure if it's for you, BUT I thought it would be a good idea,"* it instantly tells their subconscious that there is no pressure. By implying that they might not be interested from the start, it has the opposite effect. After all, we're known for wanting what we cannot have. Tell them they might not be interested in something, and they will instantly become a lot more interested.

- **Open-Minded** - This is going to work very similarly to the power phrase above. All you need to do is add this word *before* what you want to present. For example, if you were trying to get your friend to loan you their car for the weekend, phrasing your statement with the word open-minded, immediately increases your chances of them saying yes. *"How open-minded would you be about letting me borrow your car this weekend? I really need one, and mine is in the workshop."* The reason this simple word is going to work so well is that people like to think of themselves as open-minded. When you insert this word into your request, their subconscious brain tells them that going against your request is going to make them seem like they are not open-minded at all. This makes it difficult for them to say no since most people would prefer to preserve a good image of themselves.
- **What Do You Know** - This combination of words is like the final knockout punch you deliver to win any argument or discussion. Especially if you're dealing with someone who is stubbornly refusing to listen to reason because they think that they know everything already. When two people are in a discussion or argument, each person has their own opinion. This opinion is usually based on a foundation of knowledge that they have about a certain topic. Some people like to think that they know everything, and they love to appear superior. The *"what do you know"* phrase is a confident way of calling them out. Indirectly put them on the spot without being too obvious by challenging their knowledge about the subject. It can make them doubt their own opinion, and that is when you swoop in with the winning punch.
- **How Would You Feel** - This next winning combination of words can get anyone to do anything you want by playing on their emotions. Not to the point of manipulation, but just a little bit. *How would you feel if, by this time next week, you still couldn't persuade your client to close the deal with you?* How did that sentence make you feel? Chances are, that sentence probably stirred some emotions in you. A feeling of loss, almost as if you would be losing out on something if you didn't get the deal. Every

decision that we make is a decision that moves us in two directions. Pain or pleasure. This is what every decision is based on, and that is why this winning combination of words is going to work extremely well. We are all motivated to move away from anything that might cause pain. Phrase your statement right, and you will have people eating out of the palm of your hand if they believe by doing so, they are moving away from pain.

- **Just Imagine** - If someone can't imagine themselves doing something in the real world, they're not likely to do it. For example, before a woman agrees to go out with you, she must be able to picture what the two of you would look like in her head. Even men do the same thing. If either the man or woman can't see themselves with each other, they're not likely to say yes. When a wealthy person walks into a dealership to buy a Lamborghini, they don't need to think about the purchase. They're already decided on the car because they have pictured themselves driving it in their minds. By using the words *just imagine,* you can plant an image in a person's mind that gets them thinking about what it would be like if they were to go along with your request.

The way that you say these words matters as much as the words themselves. You need to be over-confident when you're using these power phrases, even if you might not be feeling all that confident yourself. The more confident you are, the greater your chances of persuading other people to sway over to your side of the fence. Your words are powerful, and you could be using them to get what you want out of life if you know how to use them correctly. Don't forget about your body language too. No one is going to be convinced in your idea if your shoulders are hunched, and you're slouched the entire time. Stand up straight with your shoulders back, maintaining good posture, and project an air of confidence. Just imagine if you did that? You would have no problems winning anyone over.

CHAPTER 3
Techniques That Tug The Emotional Heartstrings

Emotional manipulators. What is it about them that makes them so dangerous? Well, for one thing, when an emotional manipulator has their sights set on you, they are not going to stop until they have you wrapped around their finger. Their mission is to use stealth to control you and to get away with it for as long as they possibly can. The trouble with emotional manipulators is that they can be so incredibly likable. They make you fall in love with them and crave their attention to the point that we are willing to follow them with blind ignorance. Even when the signs are there, we don't want to see it because it's a hard pill to swallow. How could someone so likable be manipulating us? Are they using us for their hidden agenda? The sad truth is, they can and they will.

How Emotional Manipulators Sink Their Claws Into Their Victims

Emotional manipulators are known for playing the guilt card. Guilt can be a very powerful, emotional driver. It never feels good to feel guilty, and the manipulator is going to bank on the fact that you want to avoid this emotion. They have no qualms about making you feel bad for not helping them out, playing on your guilt, and making themselves seem like the injured party in the scenario. This is a cunning way of getting you to agree to their agenda without seeming suspicious. This sly individual will subtly play on your emotions by making you feel as though you were the selfish one, the one who didn't "care" enough to be there for the manipulator when they needed it. They would even stoop so low as to make you feel bad for prioritizing your needs over theirs. Emotions are powerful, and guilt is one of the most powerful ones that we possess. Guilt can make you do things you don't want to do, just to avoid feeling bad about the fact that you had to say no to someone or turn them down. To make this tactic work, the emotional manipulator must distort the truth and make themselves seem like the innocent victim in any scenario. They love poking on your weak spots, and in some twisted way, they delight in your misery.

They will guilt you, they will blame you, and they will shame you. They act like a martyr, subtly implying guilt by pointing out how everything they did was "for your benefit" or "because of you." Some manipulators love applying this tactic to make you feel bad enough. In doing so, they end up doing what the manipulator wanted all along. They love making other people feel bad about themselves. They play on your feelings of guilt to get what they want, and when it isn't given to them, they revert back to being the victim, hoping that you'll feel guilty enough to take the action they wanted you to all along. Guilt is the emotions that they use against you, and guilt is the emotion that they use to sink their claws into you.

Emotional Manipulation Is Emotional Abuse

There is no justifying why you would manipulate someone emotionally. Emotional manipulation, like other forms of manipulation, can be classified as abusive because of the scars and the trauma they leave behind on the victim. Emotional manipulation is a lot more common than we realize. Sometimes, this form of manipulation takes place even among those who are not manipulative by nature. It happens sometimes. We all need to manipulate for one reason or another. We don't notice because we're not paying attention. We blow things off, we let it slide because we don't want to make a big deal out of it. Emotional abuse is not as obvious as other forms of manipulation, but it is perhaps more dangerous because it doesn't get talked about enough. People don't reach out for help, and they don't know how to react or respond when they realize they have been a victim of emotional abuse.

Emotional abuse is about two things: *Power and control.* The person who is the abuser (the manipulator) will always be the one who tries to gain more power and control over everyone else. Emotional manipulation is damaging. Mostly because the victim is not always aware of what is going on. Emotional manipulators will push boundaries. They won't take no for an answer, they won't listen, and they will bulldoze their requests onto everyone else with little regard for their feelings. They fail to understand the concept of boundaries, which is why they have no problems pushing others beyond their breaking point in the relentless pursuit to get what they desire. They crowd your space physically, psychologically, and emotionally, and they care very little about how you feel about it. When someone tells them no, the manipulator doesn't listen. When you tell them that their behavior is not okay, they'll completely ignore you. Why? Because they don't care, and that is the simple truth. They don't care about anything else except their agenda. In fact, they enjoy pushing others to the limits, and they will go to any lengths to do it, including pushing past your boundaries or violating rules to do so.

They don't mind going against your wishes if doing so means they can get what they want. They may resort to behavior that includes intruding on your personal space, taking or borrowing your things without returning them, taking someone else's work and passing it off as their own, breaking promises, appointments, and even negating on agreements that were made. In some extreme cases where you might be romantically involved with a narcissistic manipulator, they could even resort to tactics that include sexual abuse or harassment, domestic violence or abuse, and even verbal and emotional abuse. The worst part of it all is some manipulators even take pride in their behavior under the misguided notion of feeling "powerful" when they see someone else suffer at their hands.

Emotional manipulators also happen to be the biggest energy drainers because manipulators are toxic. They have a way of walking into the room and bringing with them a dark cloud of negativity, which is their way of making sure that everyone's attention becomes focused on them. People who are toxic will always suck the energy out of the room and the people that they encounter too. Whether they're feeling angry, annoyed or discontent, they want you and everyone else who might be in the room to notice, and these tactics often work because people will scramble to attend to the manipulator and ask them if they're alright or what they can do to help them feel better. The manipulator then feeds off the sympathy they are receiving from others, and by the end of it all, you feel completely emotionally exhausted, and the victim will have no idea why. The worst part of emotional manipulation and abuse is that as soon as you voice your concerns about feeling confused, overwhelmed, or under pressure, the manipulator starts paying attention. They will cunningly try to sow more seeds of doubt and make you feel as if you're incapable of handling anything if even something like this seems to make you overreact. They will try to make the victim's emotions worse in any situation, and the best thing you can do is don't let them fool you into thinking you're being dramatic.

The Silent Treatment Is a Classic

The silent treatment is the worse emotionally abusive tactic a manipulator could pull on you. If you have been on the receiving end of the cold shoulder before, you will know how this treatment can eat away at you. Most people tend to believe that when someone is giving you the silent treatment after a disagreement, it means that they might need some time to cool off. The silent treatment is nothing more than emotional abuse, even after a disagreement. They are not "taking time to cool off," they are purposely trying to let you know that they're still "upset" with you. This prolonged period of no response is not healthy for any kind of relationship. No matter how hard you try to engage with them, they simply flat out ignore you, even when you're standing right in front of them. By completely ignoring you and pretending like you don't exist, they're trying to inflict as much emotional pain on you as they can without saying a word. They know it hurts you to be ignored, but they do it anyway. When you hit a nerve with someone or go against what they were hoping you would do, they might resort to the silent treatment if they are manipulative.

Why do manipulators, narcissists, psychopaths, sociopaths, or any of those toxic personalities love inflicting the silent treatment on others?

They're aiming to inflict as much pain as possible. Some tactics that you might witness under the silent treatment include refusal to acknowledge your existence, even when you walk into the room or sit directly in front of them. They could also refuse to engage in a conversation with you. When you try to talk to them, you're met with cold silence and a hostile glare. They refuse to make eye contact with you, even when you're doing your best to try and talk to them. If they do decide to respond, they'll choose to only use one or two sentences, keeping the response as minimal as possible and in clipped, hostile tones. If the manipulator is a narcissist, they might take things a step further. The narcissist takes things a step further by actually shaming and belittling you in public. At any opportunity to lower your self-esteem and make you feel bad, the narcissist will be willing to pounce. The lower your confidence, the more you will learn for validation and approval, which is what the narcissist wants you to feel. They want you to hang onto every word and continuously come back to them for their approval. It is a form of passive-aggressive behavior can make you feel crazy, and it is designed to show that they are "punishing you." The silent treatment emits incredibly toxic and negative energy when it's in play.

The silent treatment is not the best approach to take. It inflicts emotional trauma on the people you use it on. Being ostracized and treated like less than a person will put the other person on an emotional roller coaster, except this is a ride that is going to inflict psychological trauma on you that is so scarring it could destroy your confidence, self-esteem, and even your self-worth. The feeling of betrayal that someone you love could subject you to this kind of treatment lingers on the psyche, and depending on the intensity of the ostracism, the psychological effects can be hard to bounce back from, especially among young children.

The purpose of the silent treatment includes the following:

- **Making the Victim Wonder What They Have Done Wrong** - The victim begins worrying and wondering if they have done anything wrong. They can't stop thinking about it. If the victim happens to be an anxious person with a tendency to overthink everything, this approach is going to drive them crazy. They'll even start obsessing about what they might have done wrong (even if they haven't done anything). Pointedly ignoring someone is one way of inflicting pain without leaving any visible bruises. When we ignore or purposely exclude someone, research has indicated that it triggers a similar area in the brain, which is activated by physical pain.
- **To Avoid Looking Like the Bad Guy** - Since manipulators don't like any kind of accountability or responsibility, they would prefer to avoid looking like the bad guy. In a disagreeable situation, the one who keeps silent is often the one who ends up looking like the victim. One reason why manipulators love the

silent treatment is that it allows them to get away with their aggressive behavior while still looking like the victim, gaining the sympathy and attention from others that they wanted all along.

- **To Make the Victim Feel Guilty, and Scared** - The victim could be completely innocent, but when faced with the silent treatment, they can't help being overwhelmed by feelings of guilt. Sometimes, they might even feel scared. When the manipulator does this, they want to show the victim that they are in control. It is their indirect way of letting the victim know they have control over their emotions. Do what they want, and everything is right as rain. But if you don't do what they want, that's when the trouble starts.
- **To Get the Victim's Attention** - If the manipulator happens to be a narcissist, you can be sure the silent treatment is going to be one of their go-to techniques. They want attention from people around them because they genuinely believe the world revolves around them. In their mind, it is all about getting their needs met.
- **To Make You Worry About "Losing Them"** - They know they have influenced you enough to have you hooked. They know they've played their part well enough that you have become emotionally attached to them, and thus, the silent treatment is a way of "punishing" you and making you worry about "losing" them. The truth is, you're never going to lose them. They're not going to let you go when they know they can use you for their own benefit. This is another way of instilling fear in you by indirectly threatening that if you don't do what they want, they will walk out of your life. When you are a victim of emotional manipulation, you're blind to their faults, especially in the initial stages. They make you forget that they were the ones who pursued *you* and wanted to be in your life, not the other way around. Your life was perfectly fine before them, and given their toxic nature, your life will be better off without them too. But they have you fooled into thinking otherwise.
- **They Want You to Prioritize Their Feelings** - They want you to run around in circles worrying about how they feel. They want you to focus on keeping *them* happy, and they do this by inflicting the silent treatment on you whenever you do something that they don't agree with. They make you forget that no one has the right to barge into your life and demand that you worry about how they feel. Their feelings should not be the focal point of your day every day. Yet, victims of the silent treatment still find themselves doing this. The victims will be running around in circles, trying to keep the emotional manipulator happy while their own emotions are going topsy-turvy inside.

- **They Want to Use Apologies as A Weapon Against You** - The manipulator's apology may sound "sincere," but it is not. They *sound* like they are saying sorry, but what they are *really saying is* they are sorry they couldn't get you to do what they want. You will know when this technique is being used on you because they will apologize, but they will be giving you the cold shoulder for the next several days. They will "apologize," yet you still worry that something might be wrong or the situation wasn't fixed entirely. Another indicator that it was a fake apology is when they continue displaying the same behaviors that they were supposedly sorry for. When you confront them about it or point it out, they're going to deny it, of course. But if the silent treatment is still ongoing despite the apology, that is a sure sign it was fake.

Manipulative silent treatment tactics include the following:
- **When You Refuse to Talk Until the Other Person Gives In** - They will refuse to talk to you for as long as they feel like it. Usually, until you agree to give in to what they want. They will make you feel like it is your fault for not living up to their expectations. They can be very hypocritical, claiming that they would never do anything to hurt the victim while at the same time inflicting the silent treatment on their victim. Manipulators are hypocrites, which is why no relationship with them will ever be considered a healthy one. Manipulative partners will have no qualms about enforcing a set of rules which they expect you to follow to "make them happy," but they have no problems not abiding by the same rules they have set. They expect you to conform and do it, but they're not going to show you the same kind of courtesy because the rules don't apply to them. As soon as you don't live up to their expectations, they will pull the rug out from under you and leave you wondering what on earth went wrong.
- **When You Are Purposely Being Difficult** - Knowing that they have to make you work for their approval, affection, or attention feeds into the ego of a manipulator. When they know someone is groveling at their feet (not in a literal sense), it gives their ego and boost, and in the case of a narcissist, it makes them feel special. Manipulation is all about control, and nothing says control more than when someone else has to beg you for your time and attention.
- **Whey They Ostracize You** - As humans, we are naturally wired for a sense of belonging and community. It has been that way ever since the days of our early ancestors. We live in groups, we need to feel like we are part of a unit, and anything that ostracizes us or sets us apart is enough to affect our emotions. We are wired to feel the need to belong and connect with other

people, and this is why rejection never feels good. Rejection is pain, and this includes any form of rejection, no matter who it is from. Even if a complete stranger were to ignore you, you would still feel the pain since your brain leads you to believe you are being ostracized.

- **When They Throw Emotions Into Turmoil** - Since human emotions are volatile, it can throw the victim's emotions into a state of chaos when they are being subjected to the silent treatment. It increases the likelihood of mood swings and unpredictable behavior in some cases. The manipulator knows that when the victim is in such a state, they are incapable of thinking properly. All the manipulator has to do is wait until the victim can't take it anymore before they swoop in and deliver their ultimatum.

- **One Minute They Love You, the Next They Hate You** - Nothing messes with a person's mind more than this approach. The manipulator loves to put their victims through the wringer, tethering between love and hate. The relationship becomes a very frustrating one when the victim always must wonder whether you're going to love them or hate them today. They'll be obsessively worried and tread with trepidation around you because they don't know which way your mood is going to blow this time. This tactic can make you feel helpless because you don't know what you did wrong or how to fix it. Manipulators will tip the scales in their favor by creating a power imbalance in every discussion. This subtle trick is used to give them control while making you feel like you can't do anything about it. They waste no opportunity to remind you how important they are and the kind of influence they can have. Feeling helpless and emotionally miserable is how they control you into doing their bidding.

- **They Do It By Using Ultimatums** - To get you to go along with what they want, they force you into a corner by giving you an ultimatum that often leaves you no choice but to side with them. If the manipulator in your relationship doesn't like your friends, they could make you choose between being with them or giving up your friendship. They make you feel pressured into choosing them by instilling the fear that you might lose them if you don't. This type of manipulation can even occur in friendships, where your manipulative friend who might be jealous of a new friendship that you formed makes you choose one or the other. Someone who genuinely loved you or cared about you would never make you resort to such a thing. They would never put pressure on you to give up something they know that you loved, or that meant a lot to you.

- **They Start Blaming You For *Their* Problems** - They are inflicting the silent treatment on you because they blame you for their problems. That is what an emotional manipulator does. They are incapable of owning up to their own faults. You are always going to be the "reason" for their problems or why something went wrong, so they feel justified in giving you the silent treatment to make you feel terrible about yourself. Narcissists, in particular, can't bear to think of themselves as flawed or imperfect in any way. They will be the ones who always find someone else or something else to blame. This is an easy way out for them. It takes a lot more courage to own up to your mistakes, something the manipulator will never do because it would mean having to admit that they were flawed.

The one thing we need to clear about is that the silent treatment is inflicted *on purpose*. When someone uses this tactic on you, they know what they are doing. They know the kind of emotional and psychological damage being ignored can do you. This is not a tactic they use for fun, oh no, it isn't. This is a calculated move that is well thought out. The more the victim seeks their attention and approval, the more it feeds into their ego. By purposely using silence as their weapon of choice, they expect you to work out for yourself what's wrong and what needs to be done to fix the situation. Only when you have resolved it in a manner which they deem fit, then they will resume acknowledging and talking to you once again. Emotional scars are the ones that last a lifetime. Apologies can be made, but that doesn't mean the pain goes away completely. Emotional pain is capable of hitting you on a much deeper level than physical pain ever could. No matter what your intentions for persuasion or manipulation are, what you need to keep in mind is the damage that it could potentially cause, and whether it was worth it or not. When someone ignores you on purpose, they're trying to send a message that you're not good enough. Even if you haven't done anything wrong, the natural inclination is to feel guilty or wonder what you might have done to deserve it. No matter who does it, being on the receiving end of silent treatment can be mentally and emotionally damaging.

The Emotional Manipulator's Crazy Behaviors

Out of all the personality types, the covert narcissist has the highest tendency toward emotional manipulation. Now, these behavioral traits are not exclusive to the narcissist alone. Other types of emotionally abusive personalities may display some of these common characteristics too. If any of these traits resonate with you, you could have been covertly manipulating other people's emotions without even realizing it.

- **The "Word Salad" Game** - Conversations that don't make any sense are a favorite mind game of the malignant narcissist. Word salad is when a person uses a jumble of words and throws them together for no rhyme or reason with no structure, purpose, or coherence. Word salad conversations are often nonsensical, and what you're left with is utter nonsense and an argument that is unreasonable. They're just trying to confuse and frustrate you enough to the point where you eventually give up and give in to what they want when you can no longer take the frustration anymore. Attempts at disorienting and confusing you are a favorite tactic whenever the narcissist believes that they are about to lose an argument, or when they believe you are challenging or disagreeing with them. They aim to discredit and frustrate you, and the longer you stand there trying to have a rational conversation with them, the more frustrated and drained you will begin to feel. When you're at your lowest point, but you still try to stand your ground anyway, they whip out the silent treatment, ignoring you until you finally can't take it anymore and give in to them.

- **They Make You Feel Crazy** - When you're already going crazy trying to figure out what went wrong and why you're being subjected to the silent treatment, they come in and make you feel even crazier by gaslighting any points or arguments you may point out. With the silent treatment, you're already questioning yourself and feeling guilty, even when you have no idea what is wrong. Gaslighting your points will only make the situation worse. But of course, that is what the manipulator wanted all along. The "crazier" and less confident you feel, the better it is for them. When someone makes you question your sanity, it can have a tremendous impact on your confidence, self-esteem, and ability to trust anyone else. This paranoia can last for years, and the rest of your relationships are going to be the ones that suffer the consequences.
- **Nitpicking to A Fault** - Imagine if someone was always pointing out your flaws and everything that is wrong in your life. First, they point out your flaws, and then ignore you to make it sting even more. They will nitpick every single detail so much that it becomes destructive and bordering on a personal attack. Narcissists will lead you to believe you're not good enough for the impossible standards, and their comments are not meant to help you, but rather criticize you and make you feel unworthy. They make you feel even worse when they choose to ignore you after pointing out your flaws. But, a few hours or a few days later, they start talking to you as per normal, like nothing happened. This emotional yo-yo that they put you on can negatively impact your psyche in the long run.

Other Emotional Manipulation Techniques

Emotional manipulation is enough to drive anyone crazy. The worries that go on and on in your mind, day in and day out, are enough to make anyone feel like they are losing their marbles. That is what being subjected to the silent treatment will do. It makes you question yourself and worry about whether you're the problem. This is what these calculative, conniving emotional abusers want from you. The less confident you are, the easier you become as a target of their deception. It makes you desperate for forgiveness that you would be willing to say and do anything, even things you normally wouldn't do, just to get your partner to accept you again. It makes you second-guess yourself, and it causes you to doubt your self-worth, and being desperate for acceptance and love might make you become somebody that you're not. It makes you become somebody that they approve of or expect, even when you don't recognize who this new version of yourself is.

Here are the most common emotionally manipulative tactics:

- **Find A Way To Be The "Victim"** - This is the way most manipulators operate. They find a way to always be the "victim." The whole world feels sorry for them. Manipulators can easily trick the people around them into believing that they need them. In truth, the manipulator's pretend helplessness is nothing more than a ruse to mislead you into doing what they want. Pretending to be the victim is their subtle way of indirectly telling you that you *cannot* leave them, or they will crumble and fall without you. Not true at all. The only reason they want you around is that you're useful to them. They will always appear to be the "victim" because they can twist and turn their words so well. To make themselves appear blameless and innocent, the manipulator will always twist and turn your words to distort what really happened. It will always be to their benefit, never yours. Somehow, they end up making you feel like the one who is in the wrong, and you are the one who walks away feeling guilty even though you had every right to voice your discontent.
- **Appear Superior** - Snide remarks, criticism, and pedant are a few ways to emotionally manipulate your victim into believing they are not good enough. If they are exposed to this kind of behavior over a sustained period, it won't be long before it eventually begins to chip away at their self-confidence. The less confident they are, the easier they become to control. Emotional manipulators are often arrogant and narcissistic, acting in a superior manner towards everyone around them. To make you feel inferior, they will overwhelm you with data all at once, especially in the workplace, and often about subjects or pieces of the data that you don't know of, making you feel insecure about falling behind.

- **Triangulation** - Another tactic to play on the victim's emotions is to say nasty things that make them feel bad about themselves. Driving wedges between people is one way of separating the victim from the rest of their social circle. When the victim feels "isolated" from everyone else, they become a lot easier to manipulate.
- **A Blast of Emotion** - The quickest way to make the people around you feel uncomfortable enough to agree with you (depending on the situation and circumstance) is to have an emotional blow up. An outburst of emotion makes people feel uncomfortable because they don't always know how to react. When you produce a highly emotional reaction, like a burst of anger or an outpouring of tears, people will be less reluctant to ask questions and try to poke holes in your requests.
- **Project** - This emotionally manipulative tactic happens when you project an air of perfection and make it seem like other people have all the flaws. By creating a false sense of discord, you will try to make you and everyone else feel like they owe you a favor. With this manipulative tactic, you don't want to take ownership of your mistakes because you don't believe you're at fault. That is what an emotional manipulator tends to do. Project an air of perfection and let other people believe they are the ones in the wrong all the time.

Purposely Misunderstanding - If you want to make your victims feel frustrated, you need to pretend that you purposely misunderstand them. Emotional manipulators who use this tactic tend to spread falsehoods and wrong ideas about their victims. They do this on purpose to make the victim look bad. Manipulators will attempt to create confusion and misunderstanding by making sweeping generalizations and blanket statements that often have no factual basis. Exaggerations aimed at invalidating the victim's experience are how they try to maintain the upper hand against their opponents. Repeatedly telling your victim that you've misunderstood is a deceptive way of undermining their communication skills, making them doubt their own ability to. Let it go on for long enough, and they will lose their confidence to speak up for fear of being misunderstood again. This creates even more frustration in your victims by deliberately misrepresenting their feelings and thoughts until it becomes almost absurd. Instead of respecting their opinions and emotions, turn them into character flaws if it doesn't align with your own agenda. That is how you become emotionally manipulative. Weaving and spinning tales to reframe what it is you're really trying to say is what manipulators do best.

- **Flirting** - Oh yes, flirting can be considered an emotionally manipulative tactic. Some people can be naturally charming, but it is the ones who are too charming that you want to watch out for. Flirting with someone could be as simple as constantly flattering them with praise even for the simplest of items. Flirt and use charm to get what you want, and some people will go to any lengths to stroke your ego just to get you on their side. When you flirt with someone to get what you want, you're manipulating them. Be careful not to overdo this tactic, though, since once it starts to feel too much, the victims will be on their guard and think you might be up to something sneaky.
- **Intimidation** - This manipulative tactic calls for the spread of fear among the people you are trying to control. Do you notice how in a toxic work environment, there are some managers or bosses who instill fear in the hearts of their victims? When that boss or manager rolls around, it is pin-drop silence. That is what happens when you employ the use of fear as a manipulative tactic. When people are afraid of you, they will also be too afraid to disagree with you. Manipulators will try and use this tactic to instill either extreme fear or discomfort in their victim and put enough pressure on their victims until they will quickly succumb to their bidding just to escape the emotional abuse. For example, they could raise their voice when you try to push back against their suggestion. They could display temper tantrums when you try to reject their requests. They condescend, they belittle, and they talk down to you and make you feel small and insignificant. They make it clear that they are superior while everyone else is simply inferior. As soon as the victim feels small and starts to question their confidence, that is when you swoop in for the kill.
- **False Promises** - Nothing creates more stress and frustration in the victim than when the manipulator never follows through with what they promised, and then they conveniently fail to follow through at the last minute, you could be a victim of manipulation. They are skilled at "forgetting" what the promises that they made, denying that they ever said anything at all, and you must be the one who is mistaken. With no recording or documented proof to hold them to it, they pin the excuse on your poor memory, perhaps even resorting to calling you an outright liar. So skilled are they at this tactic that they make you start to doubt yourself and wonder if perhaps you could have been mistaken after all.
- **Taunting** - Keep taunting your victim by moving their "goalposts." This is another attempt at making them feel inadequate. When someone proudly tells you how they accomplish one goal that they set out to do, you'll come back with something else that you haven't accomplished. If your victim

points out how they finally got promoted or achieved the success they wanted for your career, you will come right back by pointing out how they are not a millionaire yet.

CHAPTER 4
Make Them Agree If You Want Them To

Think about a person that you know in your life that you disagree with. Think about this person disagreeing with you on a subject that matters to you. The kind of disagreement that could potentially spark an argument. Perhaps an argument that is explosive enough to end a friendship. Why do we find it so hard to get other people to say yes to what we want? There could be several reasons for that. One of those reasons is that you're not actively listening to them. While you may be "listening" to what they say, what you're really listening for is the opportunity to refute whatever they say. They are doing the same thing. Instead of listening actively to better understand each other, we're listening for opportunities to rebuke each other's claims. No wonder we find it so hard to convince people to say yes when we want them to. We've been going about it the wrong way.

Everyone is guilty of this. It's not that we are doing it on purpose, but it is because everyone has a natural tendency to prioritize their needs before everyone else's. We want other people to listen to *us*. We want them to nod along to whatever we say. But are we extending the same treatment towards them? Everything you are expecting out of a conversation, they are expecting the same thing. Most people reading this book assume they are open-minded and flexible. But, truth be told, you might not be as open-minded as you think you are. If you sometimes feel the need to resort to manipulative tactics because you feel you're not being listened to enough, then you're probably not as open-minded or flexible as you would like to believe. You and many other people out there find it hard to say yes to each other because we're not willing to change what we believe in so easily. Even when we are faced with the facts, it can be hard to change.

Change is never an easy thing. Changing our minds about something we believe is important to us will take time. It takes a lot of effort and a lot of trust to change your mind. This is something you need to keep in mind when you're attempting to get other people to say yes to you when you want them to. Just because you want them to change their minds *right now,* doesn't mean it is going to happen. Trust takes time, don't get frustrated with them if they need a little more convincing. Getting someone to say yes to you requires not only trust but also empathy, patience, vulnerability, and, most of all, it needs *courage*. The ability to change someone's mind is a skill.

There Is A Science to Saying Yes

Persuasion is a subject that has been studied by researchers for a long time. It would be nice to think that we consider all the available data before we make a decision. The truth is, our brains have a lot more to do with persuasion than we think. Your brain may have enormous power, but it also contains weaknesses, and that weakness is the fact that it can easily be influenced and manipulated. That you can be persuaded to say yes, if you know how to push without being pushy. If you think about it, that's what manipulators are doing already to get their way. They're relying on a few subconscious techniques to get almost anything they want, and they're using these subconscious techniques on you because they know how the brain works, and which emotional buttons to push to make you feel a certain way. The human brain today suffers from information overload, and therefore, it now seeks shortcuts or rules of thumb that it can quickly fall back on to make a decision.

In his book entitled *Influence: The Psychology of Persuasion* by Robert B. Cialdini, Cialdini talks about a study that was conducted on North American turkeys. Mother turkeys are extremely instinctive when it comes to protecting their young. But the reaction and care of the mother turkey are contingent on one thing: *The "cheap-cheap" sound that their chicks make*. The appearance and scent of the chicks don't make much difference to the other. On if the chicks emitted the cheap-cheap sound would the mother turkey care of it. Chicks that didn't make the sound would be ignored or neglected. The mother turkey is fiercely protective of those it recognizes as its offspring. Any sign of intrusion and the mother would react viciously to protect their chicks. An experiment was done to test the limits of the turkey's perception. In the experiment, a stuffed toy predator was pulled along on a string within the mother turkey's proximity. Immediately, the mother turkey reacted aggressively and proceeded to attack the "intruder." However, when the stuffed toy was embedded with a recording of the chick's cheap-cheap sound, the mother turkey welcomed the predator with open arms. This action is classified as a *Fixed-Action Pattern*. It is a pattern of behavior that is prevalent in all creatures.

A principle fixed-action pattern in human behavior that is well-known is the *"favor for a favor"* exchange. Basically, if you want people to say yes, you need to *give them a reason* to say yes in the first place. They need to know what is in it for them and how they are going to benefit by saying yes to you. Persuasion is essentially a psychological trick of the mind. Millions of people around the world are constantly persuading and manipulating others and experiencing great success with it too. Again, it boils down to understanding the workings of the human mind and what makes them tick. Manipulators rely on communication as their main persuasive strategy. We communicate so often that we do it almost without thinking. It is as natural to us as breathing, and many times we have found ourselves saying things we don't mean because we're not actively thinking about our communication process. It is not just the words that are being said, but the way that we say them too.

The human brain wants to avoid guilt and has a fixed-action pattern because it works in two different parts when it comes to the decision-making process. The two parts of the brain are the conscious and the subconscious mind. Your conscious mind is the adult, while your subconscious mind is like that of a child. Think of the conscious mind as the gatekeeper for the unconscious mind. It is designed to filter data before that data has a chance to reach your subconscious mind. We're constantly feeding our subconscious with data. So much of the subconscious thought process happens on autopilot. Napoleon Hill first pioneered the idea of positive thinking when he observed that the subconscious mind does not distinguish between destructive and constructive thoughts. Hill believed that the mind is capable of translating a thought driven by fear into reality as much as it can translate a thought driven by faith or courage into a positive outcome. It is up to us to make the distinction. Manipulators slip past your conscious mind with clever use of several word combinations to charm and beguile you, blinding you to their real intentions. They might even give the impression that they're brilliant, they're so charming and articulate when they speak. When the manipulator uses these words in a Machiavellian way, these words can pierce through almost everything.

Universal Rules That Coax Someone Into Saying Yes

Now, earlier, it was touched on how the human brain actively seeks shortcuts to help it arrive at a decision much faster, given the information overload we are exposed to daily. Universally, these are the shortcuts that everyone falls back on to help them decide whether they should say yes or no:
- Reciprocity
- Scarcity
- Authority
- Consistency
- Liking
- Consensus

Once you know how these shortcuts work on manipulating the mind into saying yes, you significantly increase your chances of getting them to say yes when you want them to.
- ***Reciprocity*** is the obligation that we feel to give back to others when someone has done us a favor, given us a gift, or provided a service that we are grateful for. When you're invited to a party by a friend, you feel obligated to invite them to the next party you are hosting at your house. People are a lot more likely to say yes to you when they feel like they are indebted to you. Therefore, if you want them to say yes, you need to give them a "gift" of some sort

that will make it difficult for them to reject you when it comes time to return the favor.
- **Scarcity** is a principle that works on the basis of "when you have less, you want more." This is why "sale" or "limited edition" marketing tactics tend to work so well, especially the latter. When someone is limited, your brain automatically tells you that you *must* have it because you don't want to avoid missing out. There is a term for this condition too, and it is called the *Fear of Missing Out (FOMO)*. In 2003, when British Airways announced that the twice-daily Concorde flight from London to New York would not be operating anymore because it had become "uneconomical," sales skyrocketed the very next day. Nothing had changed about the Concorde flight. It wasn't flying better or faster. The service remained the same. Sales skyrocketed because customers were now seeing it as a "scarce resource." Instill the FOMO in your persuasive techniques, and you will have people clambering to say yes to you.
- **Authority** means people will be more willing to say yes to you when they believe you are an authority on the subject. This one is easy enough to implement because all you need to do is position yourself as an expert on the subject, and they will be inclined to believe what you tell them. Do you notice how people automatically obliged to the requests of anyone who wears an authoritative uniform? They do it without even asking. This signals that it is important to let others know why you are a credible authority even before you put forth your request. Since you're probably not going to wear a uniform when you persuade them, your best approach would be to appear confident when you're presenting your facts.
- **Consistency** - People are likely to respond warmly when they can relate to the consistencies in your request. Our brains love familiarity, and the idea here to get them to familiarize themselves with saying yes to you. To do this, you need to present them with smaller requests and commitments, they have an easier time agreeing too. For example, when you start with smaller favors like asking to borrow a pen or asking your colleague to do you a favor and grab a cup of coffee for you too since they are already going out to get one anyway. This opens their mind to the idea that agreeing with you is not that difficult after all when they could easily comply with the requests you presented them with. A masterful persuasive individual would start with the smaller favors before working their way up.
- **Liking** focuses on how people are a lot more likely to say yes to you if they already like you. If they don't like you, their reluctance is going to make it very difficult for them to oblige to your

requests, even if they know it is going to be for their benefit. Would you find it easy to say yes to someone you didn't like? Probably not. The brain likes people who are similar to us, people who cooperate with us, and people who give us compliments. Before you begin your persuasion, start by seeking similarities that you can use as a way to connect with them. If you start that way, there is a 90% chance that you are going to be a lot more successful in your interactions with them. The principle of "liking" is a powerful tactic that you should be tapping into. Focus on areas of similarity that you share and direct their attention toward that as a start. Once they're warmed up and excited about having a subject they can use to connect with you, that is when you slowly ease your request into the picture. Don't forget about throwing in some genuine compliments before you get down to business.

- **Consensus** matters the most when they are uncertain or hesitant about saying yes. In general, people look at the behaviors and actions of others to help them decide what to do. For example, if you told someone that 75% of the people you have persuaded to hop on board with your idea were thrilled with the success they have had, you're pointing out what a good idea your suggestion is. This makes it a lot harder for them to resist since their brains are going to latch onto the fact that 75% of people you're influenced are already successful. They will want to be part of that number, and this increases your odds of getting a resounding yes out of them.

Why People Say No to You

There is nothing more frustrating than having someone say no when you *need them to say yes*. Sometimes, we might be so desperate for them to say yes that we end up making several costly mistakes along the way. We have all had someone say no to us at one point or another. It never feels good, and sometimes it feels downright terrible. You end up feeling frustrated, wondering what you could have done differently to change the situation. If you're wondering why people say no to you, it could be because of the following mistakes:

- **What You Tell Them Doesn't Grab Attention** - If the things you are telling them are boring, they're not going to be interested, let alone want to say yes. When you don't make a powerful impression right away, you're unlikely to have the power to persuade them the way that you need to. First impressions are made within the first 30-seconds of meeting someone. That is when you pretty much start to form your first impressions about them. If your first impression doesn't start off strong and immediately grabs their attention, they're not going to be interested in what you have to say. People naturally pay attention to those who give off an air of confidence. When you're confident, you automatically give the impression that everything you have to say is important. If you want them to say yes, it is time to start paying attention to your confidence, the way you approach others, and your body language. These are key factors if you want them to pay more attention to you when you're talking.

- **You're Too Desperate** - As much as you may be desperate for them to say yes, avoid making it obvious. People will do the opposite of what you want them to if they can sense your desperation. Your desperation could be the reason why you're coming off as too pushy or bossy at times. Plus, it is not doing your confidence any favors either. The approach that you should take instead is to appear calm and nonchalant like it doesn't matter whether they say yes or no. Adopting this approach will remind you to take a step back and give them some space to avoid coming off too strong. Present your points, but take a step back and allow them to come to you.
- **You Seem Negative** - Nothing turns people away faster than someone who gives off an air of negativity. If you think you're doing a good job of concealing it and pretending to be happy, you're probably not. That is because negativity is a very powerful, all-consuming emotion. If you are negative, it is going to show through, and this will quickly turn people away from you. You cannot present your points in a neutral, logical manner when your mindset has been clouded by negative perceptions even before you started. Your views and contributions will have elements of negativity in them, and it is going to be obvious to the listening party. Remember, they are *looking* for reasons to reject your claims. A negative pessimist is not a fun person to be around, and the last person that anyone will be seeking advice from.
- **You Sound Like You're Bragging** - Since you want them to say yes so badly, you could be at risk of making this mistake: *You sound like you are bragging too much.* Conversations tend to go south when you start humblebragging. That's a mistake to stay away from. Some people make the mistake of trying to impress others with their humblebrag, not realizing that it actually has the opposite effect. Imagine if you had to strike up a conversation with someone who proceeds to talk about how busy, chaotic, or fabulous their life is? They go on and on about how their job forces them to travel all over the world, or how they've been asked to take on the leadership position even though they would rather stay out of the spotlight. People will probably be listening politely and nodding along, but at the same time, they are looking for a

way to end the conversation. Even with the best intentions, these conversations never pan out well because it makes it seem as though you're trying to appear superior, and the other person feels inferior. Best to stick to the factual points and let the facts speak for themselves.

- **You Try Too Hard to Be Liked** - Trying too hard is just as bad as coming off too strong. When people sense that you're trying way too hard to be liked, they end up moving further away from you. People have an uncanny ability to spot desperation from a mile away. People pleasers are not much fun to be around because they give the impression of being too clingy or needy. People will stay away from you if they sense you have any of these two traits. Pulse, when you try too hard to be liked, it makes it seem like you're willing to say anything to get them to like you. That will not instill a lot of confidence in them, and thus, they're not going to say yes to you. Stay calm and be yourself, don't try too hard even if you desperately want them to say yes to you. They eventually will if you use the right techniques on them (we'll talk about that in a bit). Tone down your intensity and save your intense passion for another time.
- **You're Too Intense** - Your passion for the subject is a good thing, but too much of a good thing can backfire when you're trying to persuade others to go along with what you want. Passion is great, and it is commendable that you have such a strong belief system you're willing to stand by. But too much intensity is not the best approach to take when you're trying to convince someone to change their mind and swing over to your side. Being too intense could make you prone to arguments when someone tries to refute your points. Arguments will only drive people away.
- **You're Not Expressive Enough When You Speak** - Being too intense is not a good thing, but not being expressive enough is just as bad. Imagine having a conversation with someone who stares blankly at you the whole time. When we're trying to persuade someone, we often rely on their facial expressions and eye contact to determine how well the conversation is going. Having someone stare blankly back at you while you're trying your best to engage with them is not a good sign. While you are trying to gauge their feelings by reading their facial expressions, you can be sure that they are doing the same thing to you. If you don't convey the right expressions that support your points, you're not going to be convincing enough to win them over. When they smile, we know it's going well. If they mirror our expressions and mannerisms, it's definitely going well. But if their brow is furrowed, creased, or they simply look bored and disinterested, it's safe to say they are not interested in prolonging the

conversation right now. When you're trying to leave a good impression, don't forget to use your facial expressions to signal to them how well the conversation is going.
- **You Have A Reputation for Being Non-Committal** - This is a case of your past coming back to haunt you, although this isn't going to happen all the time. But if you're trying to convince people who happen to run in the same circles and they know a little about your history, they're going to be hesitant to say yes if you have a reputation for being non-committal. Never following through on your promises is a bad thing. Not being on time is a bad thing. Canceling with no warning is a bad thing. People will talk, and word will spread. That is why it is so important to stick to your word when you've given it because, in some cases, your past can come back to bite you when you least expect it. All it takes is for news to spread unfavorably, and your chances of being persuasive or convincing are going to double or triple in difficulty. People will be driven away by your "boy who cried wolf" reputation. If you give your word, you better be able to stick to it.
- **You Don't Respect Their Personal Space** - Unless you're with immediate family or very close friends, you should respect a person's personal space when you're communicating with them. Too close and you make the other person feel uncomfortable, too far, and you come off as disinterested. You need to pay close attention to the person you are talking to and watch for signs of discomfort. Even if you're trying to be friendly, invading personal spaces can come off as annoying, aggressive, or just plain rude. Standing too close to someone makes them feel uncomfortable because you're invading their personal space. The concept of personal space is an important part of non-verbal communication. As soon as you notice that they are not comfortable with your proximity, take a few steps back to create a comfortable enough space between the two of you. You want to make sure you're leaving at least two feet of space and not invading their personal bubble. Watch out for your personal space, because it could very well be the tipping point that lands you a new friend, relationship, or a new job.
- **You're Too Opinionated** - Being a know-it-all is not a cool thing to be proud of, even if you have all the answers to everything. Shouting it from the rooftops by being too opinionated is not going to persuade anyone to follow you. In fact, it is going to convince them to avoid you. Being too opinionated is an annoying trait because it makes other people feel dumb or inferior to you. This is not the best way to convince them to join your team. When people come to you with a question or something they want to talk about, most of the time, they just

want someone to talk to. They're not specifically looking for a solution unless they say so. If you're too busy dishing out your opinions, thinking you have the answers to all their problems, they're not going to be thrilled about going along with what you want. People don't like to be told what to do, even if they don't admit this out loud to themselves. They just want someone to listen to them while they vent their feelings, emotions, and frustrations.

- **You're Behaving Selfishly** - This is why manipulators will never have success for long. Eventually, once people realize their true colors and how selfishly they are behaving, they'll quickly turn away from the manipulator and avoid them at all costs. Nobody wants to be around someone who only cares about themselves. You will be the last person they want to agree with if you adopt this approach. When you constantly prioritize your points of view without considering how they think or feel, it shows you are only interested in fulfilling your own agenda. People don't like this, and they will never follow you once they know this is who you are. Learn to consider the opinions of others, and it will win you a lot more brownie points in the long run.
- **You Are Not Honest** - Telling lies in a bid to guard your privacy is only going to work if you're absolutely sure no one is going to find out what you're up to. No one is going to say yes to someone who is shady, and someone that they feel they cannot put their trust in. Being open, honest, and transparent in everything you say will show the other person that can be trusted. That you act with integrity and honesty, and this will help to strengthen their trust in you because you mean what you say, and you say what you mean. Trust and respect go a long way in successful and effective persuasion, and if other people can't respect you or trust you, you will be doomed right from the start with no hope of success. The minute they think you are a liar, they begin to question if they can trust you. Would you take advice from someone you don't trust? Probably not.
- **You're Not Assertive Enough** - People might overlook you if you are not assertive enough when you're trying to convince them. Assertiveness is not about being loud and getting in their faces, demanding that they listen to you. Assertiveness is being able to stand firm on your opinion while still being able to convey your thoughts and points of view in an appropriate manner if you are in a work situation. Assertiveness is about speaking in a way that they can relate to. It is the *only effective way* to make yourself heard without committing any of the other mistakes above. Being assertive and calm during a conversation will give you the assurance that you are in control of the situation,

especially when you've got your limits to guide you and let you know what lines you're not willing to cross.

Foolproof Ways to Change Someone's Mind

Maybe you've tried it in the past, and it hasn't worked. But that might be because you haven't tried these foolproof techniques to change someone's mind and get them to say *yes* when you want them to. Perhaps in the past, you were hesitant about trying to influence someone enough to change their mind without having to resort to drastic manipulation. This is understandable enough since there is a genuine cause for concern. When you try too hard to get someone to go along with you, you run the risk of ruining the relationship if it doesn't go according to plan. Hence the need for these techniques. How do you get someone to say *yes* when you want them to? By employing the following approach:

- **Don't Turn Conversations into Arguments** - Getting frustrated when someone refuses you is something we have all been guilty of. What you should do instead of present the data you have in a way that doesn't hurt or hinder their opinions. Don't make it seem obvious that you are trying to get them to change their minds. If you can stay calm and present your point logically, they will eventually see things from your point of view. After all, it can be hard to argue against logic and cold-hard facts. Staying calm is the tricky part since our emotions can sometimes get the best of us. Emotions are going to impact both parties. If the other person you are trying to convince has a lot of pride and ego, those emotions are going to make them resistant to agreeing with you simply because they want to be right. Escalating the conversation into an argument certainly won't help your cause. Always keep the conversation as calm and neutral as possible, even when the other person is starting to get emotional. Fight your urge to combat emotion with emotion. There is no winning if you take that approach.
- **Get Them to Say *Yes* as Quickly As Possible** - Start by emphasizing and keep emphasizing points that can be agreed upon as soon as you start the conversation. Throughout the conversation, keep emphasizing the points that *you* want them to agree on with you. Start the conversation strong by talking about things that you know they would agree on, like their favorite hobbies or whether they watched Game of Thrones yet. If you can start by getting them to agree with you on several points right from the start, they are a lot more likely to say *yes* when you deliver the finishing touch. This foot-in-the-door technique is actually a common sales technique used by the savviest and top-performing salespeople. You're not manipulating them too

drastically, but you are subtly influencing their minds from the start to make it seem like you're an agreeable person. When you start the conversation with topics of interest that they can agree with, it makes them like you. When they like you, they open up to you. When they open up to you, they become a lot more accepting of your ideas.

- **Don't Tell Them You Were Wrong** - Even if you are wrong, don't tell them that. At least, not unless there is a genuine need for it. Telling someone you are wrong immediately makes you seem less credible in their mind. The minute they hear you say that they are going to think they were right not to go along with what you wanted. When you tell them you were wrong, you're giving them a strong reason to combat your arguments and resist you even more. Don't give them that opportunity to topple your arguments and let the power swing over to their side. Even if you present a lot of facts and data *after* you have admitted you're wrong, it is not going to make a difference. Once their brain latches onto the notion that you're wrong and you admitted you were wrong, that is the only thing they are going to focus on. No, keep the power in your control by still presenting a calm exterior, even if you happen to be wrong on one or two points. Never let them see you sweat. No one will know that you're wrong if you act like nothing's wrong. It all comes down to carrying yourself with confidence. If you want to change their mind, you have to avoid *looking like you are trying to change their mind*. Even if you are trying to prove them wrong, don't give the game away by making it obvious. You can ensure that the power always stays on your side by being the only person who is completely aware and in control of the conversation at all times.

- **Let Them Do A Lot Of the Talking** - This is a classic mistake that trips most people up. When you're trying to convince someone, you *are not the one* who should be doing all the talking. *They are*. If you let them do all the talking, it gives the appearance that you care more about their opinion and their feelings. It leads them to believe you genuinely care about what they have to say, and thus, they will be a lot more receptive in return when it is your turn to talk. People *love* the idea that other people are interested in what they have to say. That is because most people enjoy conversations, and they want other people to know their ideas and opinions. Listening to them feeds into their head of wanting to be heard. You're going to make them feel friendlier towards you, and they will start trusting you more when you tell them something. Let them do all the talking and pay attention to them. They will reciprocate when it's your turn to talk. One crucial tip to remember here is that even if you happen to disagree with something they say, *never interrupt them* while they are talking. This is a very risky move as it could immediately lead to a change in perception about you. People don't like to be disagreed with in general, and if you interrupt them while they're talking, they're going to shut down and turn away from you. Interruptions and pointing out that you disagree with them is like a personal attack on their ego (depending on the individual in question, of course). Another thing you could do is to agree with their opinions while you're at it. Since nobody likes to feel pressured into doing anything, you'll have an easier time convincing them if you agree with their perspective every now and then. Validating their feelings lets them know that how they feel matters to you, and that you're not simply trying to cram an idea down their throat for your own benefit. The best strategy is to be patient and listen to them with an open mind. Encourage them to talk as much as possible and the best active listener you can be.

- **Make Them Believe They Came Up With the Idea Themselves** - This Jedi-like mind trick is guaranteed to get them to agree with you and say *yes* when you want them to. There is a very simple reason why this mind trick works so well. People are easier to convince when they believe that they arrived at the solution on their own. Even if it was through your gentle guidance that steered them in the right direction, let the final decision rest with them, allowing them to believe that it was their idea all along. One effective approach would be to get them to list the pros and cons and then asking them which they believe would be the best approach to take from there. If you think about it, you tend to have more faith in ideas if you were the one who came up with them as opposed to if you heard them from someone else. Instead of telling them outright *why* they should agree with you, this is by far the smarter approach to take. It is the smarter approach to make the "suggestion" and then let them believe they reached the decision on their own. People feel pride when they think they came up with an awesome idea, and this is one way of stroking their ego while you're at it. When you let them arrive at a conclusion themselves, it makes them feel like the idea was theirs, even if you were the one who suggested it.

CHAPTER 5
Under Your Spell

What happens when someone is hypnotized? We've all seen those individuals who claim to be hypnotists. We've even seen them on magic shows or performing on the streets where they attempt to hypnotize the crowd. Perhaps the most commonly used hypnotist trick that we are all familiar with is when they swing a watch in front of us, telling us to keep a close watch while they tell us our eyes gradually feel heavier and heavier. We're getting sleepy, and when they snap their fingers, we're suddenly under their spell, doing what they want us to do. You've probably seen this trick so many times that you don't think about it too much anymore. We have become accustomed to the idea that hypnotists can make people fall asleep on command, hop around on one foot, or quack like a duck if we wanted them to.

But is there more to hypnotism than meets the eye? Is there really power to be found in a soothing voice and a watch swinging in front of your face? Maybe there is more to hypnosis than the simple party trick we initially believed it was.

What Is Hypnosis

Modern hypnosis started sometime in the 1700s, and it all began with a man named Franz Mesmer. Interestingly enough, this is where we get the term "mesmerized" from. Mesmer believed in a theory called *animal magnetism,* and he was not referring to sex appeal either. Mesmer believed that every living creature had invisible, magnetic fluids that flowed through them. Mesmer claimed that he could help to cure people of all sorts of ailments by simply adjusting that magnetic flow. He would use dim lights, flashy hand gestures, and ethereal-like music to put some of his clients in a trance-like state. However, when scientists put his magnetic fluid theory to the test, they found that it wasn't a real thing. Mesmer and his research were discredited, even though some of his patients did claim that they felt better after a treatment session or two with him. Sometime in the mid-1800s, James Braid, a surgeon at the time, picked up on this research and began to study it. He used the term *"hypnosis"* to describe what Mesmer was doing, a term that originated from the Greek word *"Hypnos."* In today's modern world, some psychologists believe that hypnosis only seems like drowsiness, but in reality, hypnosis is a focused psychological state of mind. Very similar to mediation.

As a surreal concept, hypnosis has been shrouded by misconceptions and myths. People are still scared of it despite scientific research showing the connection of the practice to how the mind behaves. Hypnosis is not a recent innovation of the New Age movement that came about in the 1970s and 1980s. In the United States, at least, hypnosis was already part of the medical world's lingo back in the mid-1800s. Sigmund Freud, Pierre Janet, and Alfred Binet were some of the pioneers of this mental condition. To understand hypnotism is to understand the history of it from ancient times to modern psychologists, researchers, and physicians.

Hypnosis Through the Ages

The earliest forms of healing evidence with hypnosis is written in Egyptian Ebers Papyrus, dating to 1550 BC. Another Egyptian papyrus (Pap. A. Nr. 65) from around the 3rd century CE explains how a practitioner's hands are laid on the patient to promote hypnosis, concentration, and relaxation. Ancient cultures ranging from the Persian, Sumerian, Indian, Chinese, Greek, Egyptian, and Roman have used some form of hypnosis. The sick in Egypt and Greece often went to places of healing that are known as dream temples or sleep temples, where hypnosis was used to cure their ailments. The Sanskrit book in ancient India, known as *The Law of Manu* explains how different levels of hypnosis are used like "Sleep-Waking," "Dream-Sleep," and "Ecstasy-Sleep."

In the Middle Ages, it was believed that kings, princes, and royals had healing powers, and the term *Royal Touch* was used because it was attributed to divine powers. Before the term hypnosis was even used, it was referred to as 'magnetism' and 'mesmerism' to describe the healing by hypnosis. Paracelsus, the Swiss physician, was among the first to use magnets as a method of healing, instead of using holy relics or the divine touch. This method of healing was used until the 18th century when Maximillian Hell, a Jesuit priest and the Royal Astronomer in Vienna, started using magnetized steel plates on the body, which then became a popular form of healing. Among Hell's students was none other than Franz Mesmer, who is an Austrian physician. He began using the term "mesmerize" to explain and describe this form of healing. Mesmer soon found out that he could induce a state of trance without using magnets, and concluded (incorrectly) that he had the ability to heal instead.

The Marquis de Puysegur, who was one of Mesmer's students, soon became a successful magnetism and also the first person to produce a deeper form of hypnosis that is akin to a sleep-walking. Soon, followers of Paracelsus-Mesmer's "Fluid-ism" Theory and Puysegur started referring to themselves as *Experimentalists*. The work produced by the Experimentalists and Mesmer was a step towards the right direction of hypnotism, where it recognizes the cures that were a result not from an object or a magnet but from a different force altogether.

Meditation versus Hypnosis

At first glance, meditation and hypnosis seem like two concepts that have nothing in common. One is all about sitting calmly and trying to find your inner peace while the other is full of flashy hand gestures and elaborate techniques to try and convince you that mind control is possible. But there are similarities that meditation and hypnosis do share, and those similarities are how both practices have a certain degree of influence on our brains. Some researchers believe that hypnosis is capable of creating changes in your brain. Some psychologists even use this technique to help their patients as part of their therapy. Hypnosis is very real, but not in the overly exaggerated manner that we are used to thinking of. Hypnosis is a mental condition that has been in our world for more than two hundred years. Despite that, scientific experts have yet to uncover how our brain, use of words and actions influence and manipulate the way we do things. Meditation is one example of a form of hypnosis since you can train your mind to enter a trance-like state when you practice it. Buddhist monks have used meditation as one approach to detach themselves from their thoughts and meditation has proven time and time again what an effective tool it can be to help us practice mindful awareness.

When scientists studied the brains of Buddhist monks, they discovered that the region of the brain associated with empathy was a lot more pronounced in the monks who had been regularly meditating for years. The higher Alpha waves in the minds of these meditators reduced the number of negative emotions experienced. Studies conducted have discovered that after 8- weeks of meditation, gray matter in the brain was denser in areas associated with learning, emotional regulation, and memory processing. The amygdala, however, which deals with blood pressure and stress, experienced a decrease in brain matter.

Meditation is probably the single most important skill you can learn in a world today where stressful stimuli come at you from all angles. Not to mention that it points out the human mind is capable of change, and it can be controlled when you have the right techniques to do it. Human beings are the species with the most highly developed brain on the planet, and because of that, we're given the gift of being able to create things. We create technology. We create inventions that make our lives a little bit easier. We've helped to shape the planet into what it is today. Our brain is so powerful that we can even reshape our reality by simply learning how to quiet the mind and change our brains. Meditation allows your mind to explore this side of your natural state, the stillness that is true and pure. There are a lot of benefits to mediation. Frequent mediation can be a wonderful tool that helps strengthen their ability to concentrate. Distractions are all around us, from the chime of our mobile devices to the advertisements that flood our newsfeed when we log onto social media. Distractions stop us from seeing reality as it is, and once we stop to pay attention, we start to realize what truly matters to our happiness.

Unlike those flashy and over the top performances you might see on TV, clinical hypnosis is actually simple. Hypnosis can be defined as a trance state of mind characterized by extreme relaxation, acute suggestibility, and heightened imagination. It's not that you are sleeping, but hypnosis is usually compared to daydreaming. The idea here is that your mind is fully alert and conscious, however, the stimuli surrounding you is not acute and turned out. Your mind is fully conscious, but most of the stimuli around you are tuned out. Your entire focus is intent on the subject at hand, excluding any other thought. It is all about focusing the mind, which is why it generally takes place in a quiet space. Preferably, you would have a room with dim lights, and if you wanted, gentle music could be playing in the background. That's another similarity it shares with meditation, which also calls for a quiet environment and perhaps some soft, gentle music playing in the background if you prefer.
A hypnotist will try to get you to focus your mind. A skilled hypnotist can help you create imaginary situations in your mind. Through hypnosis, you imagine your surroundings, and it feels like it's surreal, and these images are heightened as it engages your emotions. Imaginary situations can cause real sadness, fear, or happiness, and you may even jolt up from your seat if you are surprised or scared about something in your hypnosis. The hypnotist will walk you through relaxation exercises until you reach a state of focused relaxation. When you reach this state, it means your mind has arrived at the point where you are calmer, a lot more relaxed, and thus, open to suggestions. Once you're in the state, the hypnotist can guide you through several instructions or visualizations. Could you imagine what kind of power a manipulator might hold if they had the power to hypnotize too?

What It Psychologically Means to Be Hypnotized

There is a theory called the *Altered State Theory*. This theory believes that through hypnosis, the mind is guided to a distinct state of consciousness. Like sleep, hypnosis is described as a distinct state of your brain. When you are in this state, the brain's process works differently, and you might not be aware of everything that is happening. According to hypnotism expert, Milton Erickson, people hypnotize themselves unknowingly on a daily basis. Psychiatrists trained in hypnosis focus primarily on the trance state of mind that brings in relaxation, calm, and focus. This is called deep hypnosis, and it is often related to the relaxed state of mind between sleep and wakefulness. In daily hypnosis practice, a hypnotist will have a session with you to understand your concerns, your ideas, and come up with suggestions. You approach these suggestions as if they were real. For example, if the hypnotist suggests that you drink a strawberry milkshake, you will taste the milkshake and feel the sensation of the drink going down your mouth and throat. This is 'playing pretend' but on a more intense level.

The second theory is called the *Non-State Theory*. In this theory, hypnosis is believed to be a combination of intense focus and some expectations about what it means to be hypnotized. According to this theory, the person could very well be aware of what is going on and playing along. With both theories, hypnosis is a process that is voluntary. For hypnotism to be effective, you have to be willing to listen to the hypnotist and willing to allow your mind to drift into that relaxed state. This is why a manipulator would need to gain a person's trust before they can pull off hypnotism without running the risk of looking suspicious.

Hypnosis Frees Your Mind

It's not clear yet what makes someone more susceptible to hypnosis than others. Some researchers believe that it could have something to do with a person's brain anatomy. Hypnosis is believed to cause an increase in the brain's theta waves, which is linked to the brain's visualization and attention span. Hypnosis puts people in a more relaxed and inhibited state, and it is because they tune out any worries or doubts they usually have that prevents them from keeping their actions in check. It's like when you watch a movie or read a really good book. You're engrossed in the plot, and for a brief two to three hours, you forget about whatever it is that's worrying you- your job, your family, your projects, etc. You're focused on just what's on the screen or in the book. Hypnosis affects the way that your brain pays attention to certain things, and it supports the idea that your brain enters into a state of focused relaxation. This is when hypnotism is at its optimal.

This state of focused relaxation then allows the hypnotist (or manipulator if they know how to use this technique) to come in and influence a person's mind through a concept that is called *Top-Down Processing*. The human brain processes a lot of sensory data from the world around us. Our brain has to process and interpret the data we receive to better understand what is going on. In the *Top-Down Processing* approach, the top level of data is your memories and assumptions. This can have a big impact on what you perceive with your senses. When an experiment was done on two groups of people, one group drank wine that they were told was expensive. The other group drank wine and was told that it was a cheaper alternative. They were both the same wine, but the group that thought they were drinking the expensive one said it tasted better *because they expected it* to taste better. This also explains the placebo effect. If a doctor were to give you a pill and told you it was medicine, you would believe the doctor because you trusted them. The pill could be a piece of candy that did nothing for you, yet you would still claim to feel better because you expected to feel better.

Hypnotism only works when a person is open to suggestions. When you're in a state of focused relaxation, you are also highly suggestible. This is the point where the hypnotist tells you to do something, and you'll likely embrace that idea completely. But before you get worried that they can tell you to do anything you want (such as the ones you see on a stage hypnotists' performance- getting sensible adults doing funny things like jumping frogs), a hypnotist cannot get you to do anything you do not want to do. In this state of mind, a person's expectations would be tweaked, and the way they perceive the world around them could be changed.

Hypnotism Is Not Fake?

No, it isn't. Although what you see on TV and magic shows probably is, since those are mainly for entertainment purposes. But *real hypnosis* is anything but fake, as we have already seen. It is a form of *psychotherapy*, a form of therapy where a person can be gently guided into a deep, relaxed state. When used in therapy, the therapist helps their patients to create the changes that they are looking for in their life by slowly reprogramming the mind through the power of suggestion. This is what manipulators do when they try to "suggest" that you do what they want but in a less devious way. The power of suggestion is an interesting concept. It was first researched by Faria, Bernheim, Liebeault, and the Nancy School. It begins with Father Abbe Faria, who started his research on hypnosis in India back in 1813. This Indo-Portuguese priest returned to Paris to continue his studies on hypnosis with Puysegur, and it was Faria that proposed the fact that it was not the power of the hypnotist neither magnetism that resulted in trance and healing, but instead, power was derived from within the mind of the person. The basis for clinical and theoretical work was Faria's approach in the French school known as the Nancy School, a hypnosis-centered psychotherapy school, also known as the *School of Suggestion*.

Founded by a French doctor named Ambroise-Auguste Leibeault, the Nancy School thinking was that hypnosis was a normal occurrence instigated by suggestion and not the effects of magnetism. Dr. Ambroise was considered the father of modern hypnotherapy, and he considered that hypnosis was psychological, disregarding theories of magnetism. He also studied the similarities between a trance state and a sleep state. From Leibeault, physician Hippolyte Bernheim became interested. A prominent neurologist, Bernheim observed Lieubault and eventually pursued hypnotism, abandoning medicine. Bernheim wrote about Leibeault's teachings in his own book *Suggestive Therapeutics*, offering it to the medical world as a form of science. To this day, Leibeault and Bernheim are considered the innovators of modern psychotherapy. The power of suggestion works so well for those who are able to open their mind to the possibility because once you arrive in that trance-like state, you are able to block your mind off from the worries and the external distractions that plague you daily. A similar benefit to that of meditation. Professionally, hypnosis is always done in conjunction with other forms of psychotherapy treatments.

If a manipulator could coax others into a relaxed state, they can subtly influence them to change their minds. They know that once their victims are relaxed, suggestions are easily penetrated into the mind, and when combined with persuasion, it can be a very powerful force of change. An important key point to note here is that hypnosis is *only going to work when there is an element of trust*. Therefore, before you can even try this method, you need to get the person you are trying to influence to trust you. If they don't trust you, they are not going to listen to you. It is as simple as that.

Is There A Difference Between Hypnosis, Persuasion, Influence, and Manipulation?

Yes, there is. Hypnosis is used to appeal to our subconscious mind. Hypnotism comes from a place that needs rapport, trust as well as a level of agreement and acceptance. Hypnosis, when administered and done correctly, will allow you to make suggestions to your subconscious mind. In a professional setting, hypnosis is used to influence without manipulating too. Influence is really tied to social standing or the relationship dynamic that you have with a person you want to influence. Influence often involves some form of authority or dominance over a person or a group, and this element is what moves them to have a presence or become the source of influence. For instance, a lecturer instructing their students or a judge giving an order are examples of influence. Hypnosis relies on communication to direct attention, seed ideas, and lead cognition. The aim is to lead a person into a state of altered perception.

Then we talk about influence and persuasion. Influence and persuasion are defined as the power to affect or change a person or situation, and this power to cause change is not a direct result of forcing them into making it happen. An influencer or persuader is an influential person in your life. There could be any number of individuals who are capable of coming into our lives and leaving such a deep impact that they influence us to become just a little bit better than we were before we met them. When we influence someone, it requires us to base it upon building a similar vision of the future. We need to share in that same excitement as the other party about reaching those goals and turning that vision into reality. In this way, influence differs vastly from manipulation, because there are false hope and breaking of promises that is taking place. You're not purposely deceiving them into believing in a vision that you have no intention of helping them fulfill. Persuasion and influence have the power to create positive change. With these two concepts, you are making careful observations about what works for them and what may not be in their best interest. While you're listening actively, you're still maintaining an open mind, and you're willing to share your own ideas about what you think might work for you and what you believe may not be in your best interest. This two-way communication process enables a bond of trust to form, something which can never happen when manipulation is taking place.

Manipulation is the social transaction that involves an attempt to get someone to see your point of view and to agree with what you do and what you say, and it's often in your favor. When it comes to manipulation, it often involves intent. Is the intent to find an agreement that cherishes both sides of values, or is it an attempt to find an agreement that fits in with your own line of interest? Manipulation seeks to take advantage of another person's vulnerable state. With hypnosis, persuasion, and influence, there is no underlying sinister intent. That only happens with manipulation. Manipulation doesn't take the time to justify or point out why your approach makes more sense and why the person you are trying to convince should follow it. Manipulation is bad if your underlying intentions are. As a concept, it is not inherently bad or good. There are positive forms of the manipulation taking place all around us already, except that we tend to refer to them as "influence" rather than manipulation. The term "manipulate," it leaves the impression that the other party is being forced into something against their will. Almost as if they didn't have a choice in the matter. When we use the term "influence" on the other hand, it leaves you with the impression that you're giving the other party options, and it is up to them at the end of the day to decide which direction they want to head towards. All of the above are still methods of coercing the individual to go in one direction or the other, but the only difference is manipulation is the most underhanded, devious, and sinister way of getting what you want. The biggest downside to manipulation is that relationships can fall apart and be destroyed, once people realize they have been manipulated.

Hypnosis may seem like it is complete and total mind control, another factor that sets it apart from manipulation. The truth is, however, that complete mind control is not possible, despite what hypnotists and performers who use this entertainment would like you to believe. A lot of people think that hypnosis is just used to make someone do something that is against their will, which is why a lot of people view hypnotism in a very negative light, plus it doesn't help that several movies portray hypnotism as an attempt to manipulate and control a person. Hypnosis cannot be used for mind control. Even the KGB and CIA have both experimented on the effects and uses of hypnotism in an attempt to create the perfect spy or assassin. There has been a lot of research on this but not a huge amount of proven success. Can someone hypnotize you to do something against your will? The general consensus and answer is *no they cannot*.

Hypnosis, at its very core, can be used to instill a series of feelings, images, or stories on one person and then encourage them to commit or do something that they would never otherwise consider. Manipulation uses *force, emotional blackmail, and threats* to get the same job done. Hypnosis can be used to encourage and promote a complete mind by reprogramming damaging thoughts and helping a person with a destructive attitude to great a specific plan. Manipulation doesn't care about what happens to you or how you feel. It is all about what the manipulator wants for themselves. Hypnosis can be persuasive, but it does not give control to the hypnotist. They do not have any control over your morality, mind, sense of being, or rationality.

Hypnotizing Them to Say Yes With the ABS Technique

The most powerful hypnosis technique you could implement is the *power of your word choices*. But first, for hypnosis to work, it has to be based on a few principles. One of those principles is that the person you're trying to hypnotize must *want to listen to you*. If someone doesn't want to talk to you or listen to you in the first place, it is never going to work. They have to *want* to talk to you because only then will their mind be open and receptive to what you have to say. You could use all the most influential words you can think of, but if that person has already mentally shut themselves off to anything you have to say, your techniques are going to fall on deaf ears. The second principle is congruence. Your words need to be congruent with your actions. For example, when you're using those powerful, suggestive, and hypnotic words, you must project an air of confidence as you do.

The third principle is you need to speak clearly and distinctly when you do. You have to be specific about your word choices, and each sentence you say has to be for a purpose. The fourth principle is, you must know who your audience is. What you say has to be something they can easily accept and digest. It can't be a request that is too outrageous or alarming right away, because that is only going to increase their anxiety and they won't be listening to you. Your words have to be something that they can envision themselves doing. For example, *close your eyes for a minute. Pause your reading, close your eyes, and imagine a blue door*. That is an example of a suggestion that is easily acceptable and a suggestion you can easily envision in your mind. A blue door is easy enough to picture.

Now, we come to the words to use. Words have the power to create pictures in your mind and form associations and perceptions. The power words listen below each serves their own purpose and increases in power as they are combined the right way. Words that hypnotists use have a profound effect on hypnotic power. They can evoke a soothing quality, they can provoke anger, they can income calm and resilience. It's all about power play using words. One example of a powerful word is the word "**because.**" When you're trying to hypnotize someone, you might say something like this: *You are listening to me speak, you are listening to my voice, you can relax, and because you are relaxing, you feel more at ease because you are feeling comfortable, it helps you feel relaxed.* The word "***imagine***" is also another example of a powerful word choice since it invokes visions in the other person's mind. For example, here is what you might say if you were trying to hypnotize someone: *Imagine yourself walking towards the setting sun, sitting on a beach and listening to the waves. Imagine the sea caressing your feet as it reaches the shore. Imagine feeling realized and letting go of any worry.* Close your eyes and picture that sentence in your mind. Do you see how powerful word choices can be? Your words need to *tell* the other person what you would like them to do, but not in a manner that seems too bossy or demanding.

Hypnotic power words are designed to help you achieve three things and to do it all at one go. These three things are in a formula known as the **ABS Technique.** The repetition in the themes and the words you use will make others attentive and eat up your words because these words and phrases are daily words you'd use, but they are naturally engaging. The **ABS Technique** is a conversational method of hypnosis that focuses on three key areas:

- **A**bsorb Attention
- **B**ypass the Critical Factor
- **S**timulate the Unconscious

When someone is very comfortable around you and engaged in what you are telling them, you've got their attention. You've given these words an irresistible quality that enables you to bypass critical factors and allow your clients to feel more relaxed because of what you've said to them. It's an unconscious, natural reaction. It is imperative that you gain their *attention,* which is why *Absorb Attention* is the first point in this technique. If they are paying attention to you, they are going to be entranced as you carry on the conversation while employing the other two steps in this technique. With every spoken word, their body is responding the way you want them to- positively, calmly, listening to your suggestions, and having mental clarity. Keep in mind, it's not because they are controlling how they react, rather they are letting go of their inhibitions and their unconscious mind is fed with data.

Arrest their attention right from the start and make that your primary focus when you're trying to hypnotize them. The more attention they give you, the easier it is going to be to entrance them. To gain their attention, you must emit a state of positivity. This means that you need to start with positive energy from yourself. This is important because you want to bring out the best in others, and if you do not radiate positive energy, there's very little you can do for the person you're speaking to. Positive people are so easily able to command a room or a big crowd because there is something about them that draws everyone else's attention in their direction. It is a positive energy that they radiate. Your intention should begin with wanting to do the very best for your client. Be as energetic and positive as you can. Seek their consent, don't forget to do that. Ask them for permission to touch them on their shoulders during the induction before going into a trance. You need to make them feel comfortable in your presence, and if they are willing to let you touch them, that's a very positive sign already.

The next step in the **ABS Technique** is **bypassing the critical factor**. This means you need to stop them from shutting down their minds to your suggestions. You need to bypass that mechanism so your message can slip right through. To do this, you need to gain their trust and make them comfortable. Initially, when you first meet the manipulator, they make you feel special. They make you trust them and let your guard down by making you feel comfortable in their presence. It is only when you start noticing the little signs that you realize something is not quite right. Make them look to you for the answers, and they will be under your spell.

Finally, the last step in the technique is **stimulating the unconscious mind.** To do this, *you* need to have an idea or direction that you would like the person to go to. This is where your language skills come into play. Here are other examples of powerful word choices:

- **Pretend** - It works along the same lines as the word ***imagine*** and produces the same desired effect: *Pretend that you are a great pianist and act as if you are going into hypnotism. Soon your mind forgets to pretend and start working on becoming a great pianist.* Words like imagine or pretend give the person you're talking to something to focus on, and this will start to stimulate their unconscious mind. An interesting fact about the unconscious mind is that it cannot distinguish between what is real and what is imagined. If you can imagine something vividly, your mind can be tricked into believing that it is real. This is how masterful hypnotists are able to seemingly hypnotize someone into doing what they want. When you use words like pretend or imagine, you're getting the listener to dive into their own minds and mentally rehearse the scenario in their head. They will imagine themselves doing what we ask, and if they can picture it, they'll be more receptive to the request.
- **More** - Invokes the idea of abundance in their mind, and abundance is something we all want. When we are introduced to the idea that we could have more of something, we immediately

seek it out. *The more you listen to my voice, the more you will feel relaxed, and you will soon forget your worries. The more you focus on your inner voice, the more comfortable you will feel with yourself.*

- **Every Time** - You're telling the person what is going to happen, without *insisting* that they do it. *Every time you breathe in, you will feel yourself going into a deeper state of comfort and relaxation. Every time you feel this way, you will go into a trance.* With this word selection, it is like you're indirectly telling them what will happen automatically. A reaction that can't be helped.
- **What Was It Like** - This is another phrase that invokes imagery in their minds. *Think about what it was like when you felt happy. What did you feel? How did you feel physically and mentally?* These words all seem ordinary but placed in the right context power comes out when you know how to use them. The more vivid the image is in their mind, the greater your chances of subtle hypnotizing them into saying yes to your request.
- **You** - Using the word "you" in place of their name can be incredibly hypnotic. Using the person's name too often can be a little bit awkward and uncomfortable if you don't know them all that well. Plus, using their name too often can make the conversation feel unnatural. When you use the word "you," it makes it much easier for them to picture themselves in whatever the scenario you ask them to imagine. It makes them feel like the focus of the conversation is about them when you emphasize the word "you." Once they believe that the conversation is about them, their interest immediately goes up. Before they know it, they'll find themselves hanging onto your every word.

CONCLUSION

Thank you for making it through to the end of *Manipulation for Beginners*, and let's hope it was informative and able to provide you with all of the tools you need to achieve your goals whatever they may be.

Behind the charming smile and friendly persona, a person's true intentions might not be what they seem. But manipulation is not all bad, and it can be used for both good and evil, and whatever the outcome is will depend entirely on your intention. *It is your intention that will make the difference* between whether you're manipulative or persuasive. Understanding these fundamentals of manipulation will give you a better insight into the way the human mind works. Not only will you be able to use these techniques to influence the people around you, but you will be able to discern when *someone else may be using these tactics on you.*

Whether we like it or not, manipulation happens all around us every day. Some people choose to do it, and some do it without realizing how manipulative their actions and words are. By making it to the end of this book, you're no longer in the latter category. Now that you're off to a good start at understanding what manipulation is all about, how are you going to use everything you just learned?

Finally, if you found this book useful in any way, a review on Amazon is always appreciated!

DESCRIPTION

If you had the ability to influence people into doing anything you want, would you do it?
The world would be a much happier place if everyone could do what we wanted them to, right? We often wished we could get people to do what we want, when we wanted them to. But what if you knew *there was a way* to do that? With a little subtle manipulation and persuasion?
Manipulation. It has a bad reputation that goes along with it. But truth be told, manipulation is only bad *because* of what we choose to do with it. Manipulation could be used for both good and evil. Like everything else, it is about balance and the right way to use these techniques.
It is all about mind games and mental control. When you understand how the human mind works, you'll realize how easily we can be persuaded. Manipulation, in a way, gives you the ability to control the actions and thoughts of another. There are several skills involved in pulling this off effectively, but that is why you're here. To learn everything that you need to introduce you to the world of manipulation.
To the manipulator, there is power to be gained when you learn how to control the people around you. They are constantly on the lookout for ways they can gain the upper hand over the people around them. Getting people to do what you want is a skill that can be developed. Once you understand the way manipulation works, it can prove to be a useful skill when you need it. In *Manipulation for Beginners,* these are the basics you will cover:

- An introduction into the world of manipulation and gaslighting
- The signs that *you* could be a victim of gaslighting
- Understanding who the three-major manipulative personality group are
- How to define and understand the difference between manipulation and persuasion
- Common psychological tricks used to persuade anyone, no matter who they are
- The key phrases to winning people over
- Manipulative tactics that tug at your emotional heartstrings
- Why the silent treatment is a classic but dangerous manipulative move
- How to make anyone agree *when* you want them to
- Why people choose to say no and foolproof ways to change their mind
- How to put anyone under your spell through conversational-hypnosis
- Why hypnotism is not fake and how it can free your mind
- Introducing the ABS Technique to hypnotizing anyone

The human mind is a remarkable domain, and when you understand how it works, you can get anyone to do anything, and they wouldn't even know why. If you could learn to manipulate and persuade the people around you, it is going to change your relationships and put you in a position of power when you are the one dominating and directing the conversational flow. How do you get people to say yes to you? By being the one in control, and this is where your first step begins. Are you ready to stay one step ahead of everyone else?

www.ingramcontent.com/pod-product-compliance
Lightning Source LLC
Chambersburg PA
CBHW071407070526
44578CB00002B/510